JOURNEY THROUGH LOCS

A Holistic Guide On Cultivating Locs & Self-Confidence

Jocelyn Reneé

JOURNEY THROUGH LOCS

A Holistic Guide On Cultivating Locs & Self-Confidence

Contents

"Journey: A collective set of experiences that change your perspective; a long and often difficult process of personal change and development; traveling from one place to another." — Unknown

And So The Journey Begins...

Thank you for picking up this book and inviting me along your journey! Whether you discovered me online, through my blog or YouTube channel, or just stumbled upon my writing, I truly appreciate your support!

And I want you to know that this guide was written for you.

Maybe because you're interested in learning more about locs before beginning your own journey. *Should you start with coils, two-strand twists, or interlocking? What products should you use? Will your hair still be "neat" enough for work? And how will you handle the opinions of your family, friends, or even complete strangers who feel the need to comment on your hair?*

Maybe you're already on your loc journey but feeling overwhelmed by all the conflicting advice online. *How often should you really shampoo your hair to keep your locs clean and scalp healthy? Can you mix grooming methods like retwisting and interlocking without causing damage? And what about buildup—does the popular baking soda and vinegar method actually work, or could it do more harm than good?*

Maybe you've had locs in the past and are considering restarting your journey— this time with more knowledge. Or perhaps you're simply curious about what having locs means beyond just another hairstyle.

That's why I wrote this book: to guide you through not just the technical aspects of starting and maintaining locs, but also the deeper journey of self-awareness and self-confidence.

Why You Can Trust This Guide

My journey in hair care was set in motion long before I ever stood behind the chair as a loctician. When I was 11 years old, my aunt invited me to assist her in the salon, and from the moment I accepted that opportunity, I felt a deep sense of purpose. Working alongside her, serving men, women, and children, I learned not just the fundamentals of hairstyling but the deep connection between beauty, self-awareness and confidence.

By 19, I was already defying industry norms as a hair stylist, choosing to focus exclusively on natural hair—despite skepticism from nearly every stylist I knew. Having recently returned to wearing my own hair in its natural state, I believed my clients deserved a salon experience that felt safe and empowering, so they could embrace their natural hair without judgment. To bring that vision to life, I eventually left the traditional salon setting and created a more intimate, supportive space within my apartment. At 21, during the rise of the natural hair movement in the early 2010s, I began hosting community events and meetups for women—gatherings designed to use hair care as a gateway to holistic wellness. It was at one of these events that a pioneer in the natural hair industry challenged me: *If you truly care about helping women through hair care, you would become a licensed cosmetologist.*

I took that challenge to heart. At the age of 25, I attained my cosmetology license after completing the cosmetology science program at the Aveda Institute. This program is where I deepened my expertise in scalp health, hair structures, product formulation, and ayurvedic practices. Shortly thereafter, I worked in salons specializing in loc services and completed advanced training to become a certified loctician.

Over the years, my work has extended far beyond styling locs—I've dedicated myself to education, mentorship, and advocacy within the industry. As the Digital Loctician®, I have built an online community of over 100,000 supporters across social media platforms and utilized my blog to share expert guidance on loc care, maintenance, and holistic wellness. My content has become a trusted resource for those navigating their loc journey, whether they are just beginning, maintaining, or even returning to locs.

As a former platform educator for L'Oréal's Mizani brand, I have traveled to teach professional stylists the art and science of textured hair care. I've spoken and taught at several salons, schools and hair shows, including the Natural Hair Industry Convention. I also founded an online academy, *EducationForLocs.com*, to train both professionals and consumers in the art and science of hair locking. My comprehensive *Holistic Loctician Training Program* within the academy has certified professional locticians in the U.S. and abroad.

In addition to online courses and workshops, I have also owned a salon suite, where I mentored locticians in holistically servicing clients beginning, maintaining, or repairing their locs. And to support both the education and holistic salon services, I created *Crown Elements*®, a hair care line specifically formulated for locs. Today, these products are trusted by both salons and consumers across the country.

But beyond the credentials, the most important experience I bring to this book is personal. I have cultivated my locs for over a decade, restarting the journey multiple times as I grew into new phases of self-awareness. I have felt the weight of societal expectations, the trial and error of learning how to care for locs without guidance, and the profound freedom that comes with continuously evolving my personal definition of beauty.

You can trust that this guide isn't just about locs— it's a tool for empowerment. And it's written by someone who has been where you are and knows what's possible on the other side.

What This Guide Will Teach You

There is no one-size-fits-all approach to locs, and that's exactly why this guide exists. My hope is that you can use this book as a resource for inspiration, perspective, and knowledge throughout your journey; to help you confidently and holistically cultivate your locs. So, here's what you can expect to learn:

Chapter 1: Who Defines Your Standard of Beauty?
Before you begin—or continue—your loc journey, it's important to examine the beliefs you hold about beauty. This chapter will help you release stereotypes you've learned from family, friends, or mainstream media and empower you to define beauty by your own standards.

Chapter 2: It's Not Just Locs—It's a Whole Lifestyle

Thinking about starting locs? This chapter will help you determine if they align with your current lifestyle and reveal how your daily habits, routines, and even mindset can impact your hair and scalp health.

Chapter 3: Blueprint for Strong Locs

Your foundation matters. Whether you're just starting or considering a restart, this chapter will guide you in choosing the right size, parting, and starter method to achieve the look and longevity you want for your locs.

Chapter 4: The Beauty of the Journey

Locs evolve—and so will you. This chapter breaks down the stages of the loc journey. So whether you're just starting your locs or reflecting on a past experience, you'll gain confidence to embrace each stage.

Chapter 5: Healthy Loc Grooming

From retwisting to interlocking, this chapter explores the different methods for maintaining locs, and which products to choose (and avoid) for long-term health.

Chapter 6: Wash Smarter, Not Harder

Proper cleansing is essential for a healthy scalp and buildup-free locs. This chapter covers the best shampoos, conditioning treatments, and cleansing routines.

Chapter 7: The Art of Moisturizing Locs

Moisture is key to strong, healthy locs. This chapter teaches you how to choose the right moisturizers and oils for your locs without causing buildup.

Chapter 8: Preventative Loc Care

Protecting your locs is just as important as maintaining them. This chapter provides strategies to prevent breakage, combat buildup, and keep your locs thriving for years to come.

Chapter 9: Setting Intentions for Your Loc Journey

Whether you're inspired by someone else's locs or wondering if yours will ever "look right," this chapter will help you navigate loc envy and embrace your unique journey with confidence.

As you'll soon discover, locs can teach you patience, resilience, and self-acceptance—but only if you allow yourself to trust the process.

So take a deep breath, release expectations, and open yourself to the journey ahead.

"We cannot love or hate something about another person or the world unless it is already inside of us first."
Deborah Adele, The Yamas & Niyamas

CHAPTER ONE

Who Defines Your Standard of Beauty?

How do you know you're beautiful?

More often than not, this question is answered for us, not by us, long before we are even old enough to think about it. Starting as early as infancy, in very subtle ways, we are bombarded with society's criteria for beauty. This idealistic standard of beauty can be seen in toys and tv shows, and felt through the comments made by our favorite aunt or well meaning grandmother. But what does it mean when this standard of beauty excludes the way you desire to show up in the world? What happens when the way your hair grows from your scalp doesn't align with what's been named beautiful? For me, these questions came to life through my journey with locs.

"Do you really want to walk around with your hair lookin' nappy?" This was the first comment that I heard when I told my grandmother that I was preparing to start my loc journey. Even though this was my second summer wearing my natural hair, my family still did not approve of my choice. Sure I may have shocked them, nearly two years before, when I took a pair of scissors and chopped off all the relaxed hair on my head the

night of President Obama's Inauguration. My biggest offense, however, was not that I cut my hair, it was that I mistakenly thought what I cut off was "just hair".

When I returned to my natural hair, I also made the decision to cut ties with many of the habits and lifestyle choices that had been ingrained in me since childhood. My daily hairstyling routine was no longer about silkening my long, relaxed hair. Instead, I tossed my combs and brushes to use my fingers for shingling my teenie-weenie afro. I became hypervigilant about product ingredients and had no concern for tact when sharing the facts I learned— often ruining the experience of someone's favorite product or meal with a *"Did you know that...?"* fun fact. Nearly every chance I got, I reminded my family that what they put on their bodies impacted their well-being just as much as what they put in them. As a result, my family was sick of me—and they made sure I knew it.

I felt like the black sheep of the family. And I believed this isolation had everything to do with me no longer embodying their expectations of "socially acceptable" hair. I became aware of a deeply rooted belief within my family—and, honestly, within our culture at large: beauty, especially when it comes to hair, is to be measured by European standards. Hair is not to be viewed as an outlet of personal expression or even personal strength, for that matter.

Perhaps you remember your mother dragging you along to the hair salon to have your hair straightened for a special occasion. Or maybe you can recall hearing that your curls were "hard to manage" or "wild." These messages, even when well-intended, start to form an internal narrative during childhood. They plant a seed of self-criticism that can blossom into a belief that our natural beauty needs to be "fixed" in order to be acceptable.

Even now, when I think back to the times my younger sister and I went to the hair salon before major holidays and family events, the scorching scent of burning hair is the first thing that comes to mind. I can still see us sitting in the salon chair, holding our ears and tensing our shoulders—hoping to avoid accidental burns from the hot pressing comb while eagerly awaiting the transformation. I can recall the excitement we felt when finally being turned toward the mirror; followed by praises for the beauty that had been bestowed upon us—achieved by taming our "nappy" hair. This moment speaks to a larger truth: this is more than a personal memory—it's a shared experience, a collective devaluation of natural beauty for countless little Black girls.

I believe that this early conditioning, teaching young girls that their "best" look is realized only when their natural hair is straightened, perpetuates the deeply rooted racism and colorism within our society. As does the preference for a looser curl pattern particularly when it is associated with being "easier to manage" and requiring less effort to straighten, thereby earning the label of "good hair." While at the same time, tighter curl patterns are stigmatized as being "kinky," demanding more detangling, stretching, and heat to conform to a straightened state. And it's no secret that all of these efforts are undertaken to emulate the European aesthetic, which has historically been upheld as the standard of beauty.

I grew up internalizing these beauty standards without ever realizing I had the choice to challenge them. From the age of five through my early teenage years, my mother had my hair chemically straightened with a relaxer. By middle school, I wore it straight every day—in a style that flowed down my back, just above my bra strap. At the same time, I was addicted to sugar, rarely exercised (so I wouldn't sweat out my relaxer), and, according to my medical records, I was overweight. But I didn't accept that label because you couldn't tell me I wasn't a thick video vixen. Which is also why I stayed committed to regular hair appointments, every six weeks, to get my fix of "creamy crack." Because even a half an inch of my natural hair texture was "too kinky" and unmanageable—or so I had been taught to believe from an early age.

It saddens me now to think of the countless times I sat silently in the chair at the salon with a chemical relaxer burning away any trace of my nappy roots. I wouldn't dare say that it was burning my scalp or that it hurt badly and I wanted to wash it out. Because too often I'd sat in that same salon chair and heard the stylists telling other women *"beauty is pain"*; and I wanted to be beautiful. So the longer I sat in pain to allow the relaxer to straighten out my naturally curly hair the better. And the evidence of how beautiful I had become was measured, not by my reflection, but by how many scabs I found on my scalp the next morning. Following each relaxer session, I would look in the mirror, and comb through my limp but now "easy to manage" hair. When my comb caught on a scab, I'd wince in pain from the tenderness in my scalp but whisper to myself, "this is what it takes to be beautiful." Suffering through relaxer after relaxer to show up with Aaliyah-inspired hair was my norm. I did not realize how damaging my beauty regimen was because I looked like everyone else around me. But more importantly, I was striving to look like the women on television— none of whom wore natural hair or locs. It wasn't even until I was away at college that my unhealthy "hair care" practices were questioned, because like many young girls much of what I learned about beauty came from within my childhood home.

And yet, despite all of the societal pressures and familial expectations that shaped my definition of beauty, what led me to start my journey with locs was curiosity. One evening, during my junior year of college, I was asked two simple, but very loaded, questions: *"Why do you always wear your hair straight?"* and *"Why do you choose to put a chemical relaxer in your hair so close to your brain?"*. My immediate reaction was defensive: *Wasn't it obvious? I wear my hair straight and endure relaxers—and chemical burns—every six weeks so that people think I'm beautiful as soon as they see me.* But at that moment, I couldn't bring myself to say those words out loud. I was speechless. I had never truly acknowledged that belief to myself, let alone anyone else. What made it worse was that, for as long as I could remember, my hair had been relaxed—so I had no idea what my natural curl pattern even looked or felt like. This was the first time that my beauty practices were challenged and it made me stop and look at my reflection in a different light. That line of questioning and curiosity gave me the permission I didn't know that I needed to stop comparing my beauty to the woman next to me; and to no longer look to tv, magazines, or commercials for the definition of beauty. For the first time in my life, I began to believe that I could form my own definition of beauty— set by my own standards.

However, redefining beauty for myself was not as easy as it may sound. Not only did it involve getting to a place where I viewed my reflection as beautiful, I also had to learn to treat myself with love. But for the majority of my life "love" was just a feeling. As long as I felt that I was being beautiful it equated to self-love. However as bell hooks shares in *All About Love: New Visions* "love and abuse cannot coexist." How could I say that I loved myself while constantly subjecting myself to scalp burns in order to be named beautiful. How could I be in relationships with people who told me that I looked ugly with short hair or that my natural hair was not my best look while in the same context telling me that they loved me. I had to face some hard truths and sit with the uncomfortable emotions that had been keeping me from accepting and embracing my inherent natural beauty.

Cultivating A Personal Definition of Beauty

I believe my first set of locs were not chosen based on the recommendations I'll share with you in this guide—such as aligning with your lifestyle or having a clear understanding of how to properly care for them. Instead, I chose Sisterlocks™ because they felt like the safest option. The little research I had done at the time revealed that Sisterlocks™ were designed to mimic the aesthetic of relaxed hair; often giving frizzy hair a tamed, sleeker appearance. And, deep down, I had hoped my family would approve of them because they would look neat. But in hindsight, I realize I subconsciously chose Sisterlocks™ because they aligned with the traditional beauty standards I held from childhood.

I wore Sisterlocks™ for two years and learned several valuable lessons along the way. One lesson in particular stands out. Shortly before combing out my Sisterlocks™, during a multi-day training to become certified in offering Sisterlocks™ services, I recognized that I had been seeking validation through my hair. Imagine being in a training room where every woman there had been wearing Sisterlocks™ for years—some with locs cascading down their backs, others with lengths reaching their tailbones. And despite receiving numerous compliments and engaging in conversations where other women praised your hair, you felt an unsettling sense of inferiority. Before stepping into that room, I truly believed I had won the battle against European beauty standards by locking my hair and rejecting societal norms. But the truth was, I was still playing the game—I had just advanced to another level. I was no longer competing against the blonde, sleek, straight hair European standards. Instead, I found myself in competition with women who shared my skin tone, hair texture, and features. I had hoped this training experience would be affirming. Instead, the voices of comparison and unworthiness had crept in. Rather than seeing the beauty in myself that I so easily saw in these women, I doubted myself. I questioned how I could possibly compete.

I fixated on superficial flaws—my texture not being *kinky enough,* my locs having *too much frizz,* and my hair taking *too long to lock* compared to the women at the convention. Externally, my hair declared freedom, yet internally, my mind was still trapped. Rather than standing in my power, I gave in to self-criticism and shrank within myself. And no less than a month after that experience, I removed my Sisterlocks™, hoping it would bring relief. But it didn't. Removing them didn't free me from the negative self-talk that was living rent-free in my mind.

With my self-confidence shaken and my perception of beauty faltering, I knew I needed to return home. Not my childhood home—but home within myself, where I felt safe and loved. Those feelings were strongest when I first started locs, so I knew that was where I needed to begin.

As I embarked on my second set of locs—traditional locs this time—I found myself curating an album of screenshots featuring other women with locs. This album became my "loc goals," a visual blueprint for what beautiful locs should look like. I felt that I needed to achieve that standard in order to define myself—and my locs—as *beautiful*. No matter what others said about my locs, I measured its beauty against the images in my phone. I used their aesthetic to construct my beauty standards, just as I had been taught to do as a child. Subconsciously, I still believed beauty existed outside of me rather than within me.

So, I backcombed and tangled my curly hair into submission to form the foundation of this new set of locs. I wasn't willing to let my hair evolve naturally—I needed results now. To project an image of perfection, I coated my hair with unnecessary products to mask my frizz because any sign of frizz meant my locs weren't well put together. Every moment I looked in the mirror it was to count the ways my locs did not measure up to the images in my phone. When I wasn't comparing myself, I was searching online for ways to "fix" my hair. *It was exhausting!*

So, once again, I welcomed the same curiosity that led me to stop relaxing my hair to push me towards uncovering the beauty in my reflection.

What was it about other curl patterns that felt more desirable?

Why are locs with less frizz more ideal than my frizzy roots?

Did the length of time that it took my hair to lock mean I didn't have enough ethnicity in my roots?

Were social media likes and shares really the only measure of beauty?

Why am I not enough?

Questioning the negative self-talk that echoed in my mind every time I looked in the mirror or saved another screenshot for my *"loc goals"* album was the first step toward reclaiming my self-confidence. Asking myself these questions—sometimes in the moment, other times after scrolling social media for hours—helped me realize that it wasn't my voice delivering the criticism. Somewhere along the way, I had internalized the belief that *I was not enough.* That no matter how I wore my hair, I would never be enough *as I am.* This was the belief that was holding me back from my freedom. I needed to unlearn it. I needed to remind myself that I deserved to be free. I needed to face the doubts of my own self worth head on.

After three years of measuring myself and my current set of locs against someone else's beauty standards, I combed them out. But I knew I would restart my loc journey immediately—this time with intention and awareness. *They say the third time's a charm, right?*

What began as a personal exercise in decolonizing my thoughts became the key to unlocking my self-confidence—and inspiring thousands of others. I started my third set of locs with the belief that I could become my own loc goals. And what better way to do that than by adding my own image to the 'loc goals' album? I began sharing selfies and documenting my loc journey online—not for validation, but for self-expression. I experimented with color, dyeing my locs nearly every shade imaginable before finally settling on emerald green. I challenged myself to post daily photos of my locs and document my journey, free from comparison or judgment. Over eight years, my locs grew past my lower back, remaining healthy, buildup-free, and strong. Through this practice, I discovered a powerful truth: **beauty is wellness and self-expression is at the core of self-confidence.**

Challenging the Stereotypes About Locs

When you make the decision to start locs you too will be challenging the societal norms of beauty that most people, including family, friends and other people of color are not used to seeing. You will be wearing your hair in a way that immediately speaks for you without you having to say a word. To some, your hair will say "I don't care about my appearance or how I look in public"; and to others your hair may scream "I do drugs and I am rebellious". Many of these stereotypes, particularly in America, are a result of how locs were introduced to the country.

According to *Hair Story: Untangling the Roots of Black Hair in America*, the term "dreadlocks" originated from Europeans noticing the matted hair of enslaved Africans and describing it as "dreadful." This is one reason I prefer the term "locs" instead of "dreadlocks" as the latter carries the negative connotation from which it was derived. Fast forward beyond slavery to the 1970s, when Bob Marley, a Jamaican musician, was introduced to America. He quickly became not only a musical icon but also the cultural archetype for individuals with locs. Through his music, he shared powerful messages of empowerment for Black people, with songs like *"Get Up, Stand Up [for Your Rights]"* and *"Buffalo Soldier."* Regrettably, due to widespread ignorance, many Americans began stereotyping people with locs as marijuana smokers or radical freedom fighters. And despite Bob Marley's popularity dating back more than 50 years, many of these stereotypes still persist today.

People still make assumptions about people who wear locs: that they're unprofessional, unclean, or even uneducated. Television, magazines, and now social media continue to uphold and amplify these stereotypical narratives. Even as representation has improved, it's often very superficial, failing to challenge the Eurocentric norms that have historically shaped how beauty is defined. Think about the assumptions and labels our hair often carries. In professional environments, sleek, straight hair is often associated with competency, while textured hair or locs are seen as ignorant. These stereotypes play a large role in how society views people of color and often how we perceive ourselves. And unfortunately these stereotypes don't just influence public perception—they often become internalized, shaping the way we see and speak to ourselves.

But one of the lessons that I had to learn as I embarked on my loc journey was being open to hearing criticism without automatically reacting to it or agreeing with it. Comments like *"Why would you want to be a nappy headed girl?"* and *"Do you really think you will get a job looking like that?"* were freely shared the moment I stepped into a room. It took a lot of unlearning and self-discovery for me to find the strength within myself to recognize that their comments and judgements were not directed at me, but were truly reflections of how the person that shared them viewed themselves.

This realization, along with countless others, surfaced when I decided to view my locs as a teacher rather than just another hairstyle. Instead of following the usual stylistic approach, I embraced a more holistic path—examining my thoughts, practices, beliefs, and relationships beyond the traditional mindset of doing things simply because "that's how it's always been done." Far too often, we shackle ourselves to the opinions, expectations, and beliefs of others. But I knew I deserved freedom from the chains of society's long held European beauty standards and the opportunity to reconnect with my personal truth— so do you. So, I'll ask you again, *"how do you know you're beautiful?"*.

This time, take a moment to sit with that question, unpack the beliefs you've carried, and reclaim a definition of beauty that makes room for your full, authentic self.

"Empowered are those who remember who they are even when circumstances would tempt them to believe otherwise."
Marianne Williamson, The Law of Divine Compensation

CHAPTER TWO

It's Not Just Locs— It's a Whole Lifestyle

Beginning the journey with locs is more than a hairstyle choice; it's a lifestyle and mindset shift. In fact, you will often hear that locs and commitment are tied together. I believe this is because the decision is that impactful. And as with any major commitment, starting locs requires intention and careful consideration. Mindfully starting your loc journey will help you to avoid the frustrations and regrets that often come from rushed or uninformed decisions. This chapter will guide you through the necessary lifestyle considerations while also helping you decide whether to start your locs yourself or seek the expertise of a loctician.

Lifestyle Considerations

When it comes to locs, I strongly advocate for you taking a holistic approach that considers your entire well-being, not just your hair. This involves a thorough evaluation of factors such as your level of physical activity, current stress levels, diet, and budget. Each of these factors plays an important role in determining the best type of locs for you. Let's explore each lifestyle factor so that you have a clear understanding of how each area can impact your loc journey.

Physical Activity

I recall a consultation I had with a new client who was extremely frustrated because her locs were always frizzy and her growth was unruly. In her corporate profession this made her feel very uncomfortable about her appearance. Unfortunately, the stylist that started her locs did not ask about her lifestyle or take into consideration that she was an avid cyclist that often sweated under her helmet.

To address her concerns, I had to restart her locs completely. She needed to shift to a foundation and regimen that was more appropriate for her lifestyle in order to keep her locs together through regular shampooing and exercising. This change cost her months of progress and the expense of paying twice for starter locs, but it could have been avoided upfront with lifestyle considerations. I encourage you not to settle for simply starting locs, but instead make informed choices so that your locs compliment your physical health and wellbeing.

For many of us, exercising will cause our scalp to sweat— and sweat does not mix well with locs. When excessive amounts of wetness, like perspiration, frequently comes in contact with new locs it can cause them to frizz, unravel, or develop unpleasant odors. Thankfully, you don't have to sacrifice your loc goals for your fitness aspirations, but you do need to plan accordingly.

In order to avoid buildup, odors, and the frustration of restarting your locs each month, you will need to take extra precautions. For instance, if you enjoy running and sweat heavily on your scalp, you'll want to tie your locs down before working out and ensure they are fully dried afterwards to minimize frizz. Additionally, applying a refreshing moisturizer after workouts can help eliminate odors in your locs. It's also important to shampoo regularly. Oftentimes, you'll hear that locs only need to be shampooed once a month, but that is a myth—especially if you sweat heavily in your scalp. And it's to be expected that frequent washing can present challenges in maintaining the neatness of your locs— we will discuss more about loc grooming techniques in chapter 5. So, if you intend to introduce more physical activity into your life or currently have an active lifestyle, you should take into account the ways in which it will impact your hair care.

Stress Management

If you find yourself dealing with a lot of stress, it is best to wait until you have it under control before starting your locs. From my professional experience, I have seen that stress-induced weakness in locs can create a troublesome cycle: stress leading to thinning, thinning leading to worry, worry leading to more stress, and ultimately, breakage of the locs.

An example of this vicious cycle was a client who insisted on starting her locs despite being in the chaos of wedding planning. Shortly after she began her locs, her roots started to thin, and she experienced breakage everywhere. Naturally, her concern for her locs caused her even more stress, and her locs suffered— barely growing and hardly locking until she jumped the broom. Once the wedding was over, her hair loss almost miraculously resolved itself. New hairs began to sprout, and her roots started to thicken.

You could replace wedding planning with job loss, grief, or any number of life challenges—it could happen to anyone. For that reason, stress, while seemingly a normal part of life, should be managed before starting locs to avoid it manifesting into physical symptoms like hair loss, breakage, or slow growth. Taking care of your stress before starting locs is like ensuring the foundation of a house is strong before building the rest.

To counteract the effects of stress, I strongly recommend incorporating mindfulness practices into your daily routine, such as meditation, yoga, walking, and journaling.

Diet & Hydration

Unlike loose hair, you can't hide scalp concerns with products when you have locs. Your dietary choices and hydration levels are always on display. So, you'll need to address these issues from within. For example, loose hair will allow you to mask a flaky scalp with oil, but excessive oil application can lead to product buildup in locs, making it a problematic remedy.

Instead consider adopting a holistic approach to your eating habits; strive to consume a balanced diet with a mix of proteins, carbohydrates, and healthy fats while avoiding processed and sugary foods. A well-balanced diet not only supports the strength of your hair but also supports the natural oil production in your scalp, which contributes to healthier locs.

Water is also an essential component of maintaining healthy locs. Many of us underestimate the amount of water our bodies truly need to efficiently function. When we are dehydrated, not only does our scalp become dry, it can also lead to flaking and itching. Drinking enough water prevents dehydration-related issues such as dry hair and scalp concerns; as well as overall fatigue. Well-hydrated locs are also more likely to maintain their moisture balance, resulting in improved softness and overall appearance.

Budget

When budgeting for your locs, most people immediately think about "saving money"—deciding whether to do them at home or take on the expense of salon services. If you choose the salon route, you'll need to account for the costs of installation, monthly grooming, and ongoing hair treatments. However, I make it a priority to discuss the "investment" involved in starting locs. When shifting the perspective from "cost" to "investment" it is a practice in mindfulness. You deserve to see yourself as someone worthy of more: more care, more time, and more consideration. Speaking in terms of "cost" can unintentionally reinforce the belief that spending money on your hair puts you at a deficit. In reality, investing in your hair care is a valuable practice that contributes to your overall wellbeing and self-esteem.

As a salon owner, I witnessed the transformational impact of investing in your hair. On the surface, it may have seemed like an unnecessary expense to visit a salon, especially for those dealing with financial struggles. However, those who sit in a salon chair often leave with their joy and confidence renewed— which is a priceless experience. The hair salon, especially when being serviced by a holistic loctician, serves as a space for restorative conversations and often acts as a reminder that you deserve abundance while discouraging thoughts of scarcity. While dedicating your time and effort to maintaining your own hair may save you a few dollars, having your locs tended to by a professional is a practice in investing in your wellness.

Granted, whether you decide to seek professional care or go the do-it-yourself (DIY) route, you will be faced with the cost of products. Typically, the products offered in salons are more expensive than those available at your local store. These are often professional-grade products, carefully selected and tested by your salon professional, to ensure they promote your hair health while you're away from the salon. On the other hand, when you choose to DIY, you are left to figure out the best products for your hair on your own. This often involves spending a considerable amount of time researching online, purchasing products, and working through trial and error.

Choosing Between D.I.Y. or Professional Services

Aside from the budget there are several other factors you should take into consideration when deciding whether to embark on the journey of cultivating your locs independently or entrusting their care to a skilled loctician. Let's explore the advantages and drawbacks of each option.

Choosing to DIY (Do It Yourself)

Taking control of your loc journey can be incredibly liberating and empowering. Doing it yourself allows you to save money and create moments of self-discovery that would not happen if someone else were to lock your hair. However, DIY-ing also requires intentional awareness and effort to properly care for and maintain your locs.

I can speak from experience because my second set of locs were cultivated entirely by my own hands. Initially, I felt very proud and resourceful starting my own locs, especially since this was long before I became a loctician. I researched various starting methods, sizes, and techniques to give myself what I thought were the best possible results. Then, on December 12, 2012, I stood in front of my bathroom mirror to meticulously create uniformly square parts for my loc foundation. Spending hours starting my locs motivated me to care for them and hold myself accountable for weekly shampoo sessions and monthly grooming.

Fast forward one year into this journey, I was doing everything possible to remove the product buildup I had caused by experimenting with the wrong products. This buildup was a major setback, leaving my locs dry and brittle. Shortly after I managed to remove the product buildup, I encountered another issue. Just as my hair had finally started locking and had grown past my shoulders, I became self-conscious. I was uncomfortable because my locs started to look very "scalpy." Unfortunately, I discovered too late that the square parts I had meticulously created for my foundation were not ideal for my hair texture; and would require me to remove my locs in order to restart with a more appropriate foundation. Had I sought professional guidance from the beginning, I could have avoided the scalpiness and buildup, saving myself three years of time. Despite this experience, I still firmly believe in the advantages of DIY. However, I emphasize the importance of understanding the locking process, and knowing how to choose and use the right products before starting your own locs.

Choosing Loctician Services

Working with a professional loctician can ensure that your locs are properly started and maintained. A loctician can offer personalized advice based on your hair type, texture, and length while also providing solutions if issues arise. However, this option comes with higher costs and the challenge of finding a loctician you trust.

It is the unfortunate reality, at least at the time of writing this book, that the salon industry lacks standardized regulations for locs. In fact, in many states, there is no requirement for licensing expertise in textured hair or locs, allowing anyone to market themselves as a "loctician" without formal education or training. This lack of regulation creates a significant gap in qualifications, which often results in "professionals" doing more harm than good.

One example that immediately comes to mind involves a woman who visited my salon for a new client consultation. I began the consultation as I usually do, asking about her motivation for choosing my salon. Her response was so unexpected. Tears began streaming down her face, and before she spoke, I could feel the emotional weight she carried.

She proceeded to share a traumatizing encounter at the previous salon where she had begun her loc journey. The stylist there had discouraged her, insisting that her hair was "too soft" to form locs and expressing doubt about the end result. Despite this negativity, and motivated by the challenges she faced managing her loose natural hair at home, the woman decided to move forward with starting her locs anyway. The stylist coiled her natural hair and strongly advised against letting water touch it until her locs had fully formed.

Fast forward eight months, and the consequences of this misguided advice were severe. The woman had not shampooed her hair since the day her coils were started. This neglect led to an inflamed scalp, widespread dandruff, and significant hair thinning. When I asked her why she hadn't shampooed her hair, she confessed that fear, instilled by the stylist's advice, had paralyzed her from taking action to properly care for her hair.

I wish that I could say that this was the only interaction I have heard like this; but that couldn't be further from the truth. Countless clients and members of my online community have shared similar stories of damage caused by poor advice from so-called "locticians."

With that being said, if you do choose to seek professional support, I strongly recommend evaluating the loctician's experience and qualifications. Always schedule a consultation before committing to any services, and ask detailed questions. Here are a few questions that you should include in the conversation:

1. What methods of starting and maintaining locs do you specialize in, and which do you recommend for my hair type and lifestyle?
This helps you assess their versatility and whether they're customizing their recommendations for you or just offering a one-size-fits-all

service. Refer to chapter 3 for details on loc starting methods.

2. Can you walk me through your sanitation protocols?
You are looking for a professional that cleans, disinfects, and sanitizes their tools, including combs and clips. Clean tools are a sign of a professional who prioritizes your safety and wellbeing.

3. How do you assess hair health before recommending a service?
This will reveal whether they consider the condition of your hair at each visit or rush into services or styling.

4. Do you offer guidance on at-home grooming and product recommendations between appointments?
A hair care professional wants you to thrive in between visits and will share education with you to support your loc journey, not just charge you for a service. Refer to chapter 7 to learn more about products and routines for at-home care.

5. How often do you recommend I come in for loc grooming, and what would a typical grooming schedule look like for me?
This will help you to understand whether their recommended level of care aligns with your lifestyle, budget, and hair goals. Refer to chapter 5 to learn more about loc grooming, suggested schedules, and grooming products.

6. Do you have experience with loc repairs, combining locs, or removing buildup. And can you share how you typically handle those services?
This will give you insight into their proficiency with advanced techniques and their ability to support you long-term should you encounter any issues as your locs evolve. Refer to chapter 8 to learn

more about preventative loc care practices.

Also, inquire about their formal training, request photos of their work, and confirm that they have experience working with hair textures and types similar to yours.

Preparing Yourself for the Journey

Ultimately, the decision to DIY or find a loctician for care will be up to your personal needs and circumstances. But, before you even come to that decision, you will need to determine if locs truly fit within your lifestyle. I have found that the best way to answer that question is through self-reflection. Take time to consider the following questions:

1. Am I okay with adjusting my hair care routine, including more frequent shampoos or grooming sessions?

2. Do I have the time and patience to learn and maintain my locs on my own?

3. Are there any scalp conditions or sensitivities I need to manage before starting my loc journey?

4. Is my current diet balanced, and am I drinking enough water to promote a healthy environment for my hair and scalp?

5. Am I prepared to manage stress effectively to avoid its negative impact on my hair and health?

6. Do I have realistic expectations about the time it takes for locs to mature and the patience required to embrace the process?

7. Am I prepared for the criticism I may experience during the early stages of locs? How will I handle people's reactions to the frizz and awkward lengths?

8. Am I financially prepared for the cost of maintenance appointments and the products required?

9. Is my budget flexible enough for regular or occasional professional services?

10. What are my long-term goals for my locs in terms of length, style, and overall aesthetic?

11. Have I thoroughly researched or consulted a professional loctician about my future loc goals?

12. Do I feel confident in my ability to commit to this journey?

Taking the time and space to explore these questions will help shift your mindset toward cultivating healthy locs with intention. It will also encourage you to prioritize your self-care needs as you prepare for this transformative experience.

I understand that, for some, the commitment to locs is centered on permanence—the idea that once you start, you can't change your mind—which can feel intimidating. To that belief, I say: give yourself grace as you embrace this journey. Cultivating healthy locs is a marathon, not a sprint, and you always have the freedom to change your mind. For others, starting locs represents freedom from the constant maintenance and unpredictability of loose natural hair, making you feel eager to dive into your loc journey headfirst.

However, as I've shared, evaluating your lifestyle and making an informed decision about starting locs can save you from unnecessary frustration and regret. Also, regularly assessing how your lifestyle intersects with your loc journey will ensure that your hair care practices align with your overall well-being. By considering factors such as your physical activity, stress levels, diet, and budget, as well as weighing the pros and cons of DIY versus professional loctician services, you will be better prepared to navigate your loc journey with confidence.

Remember, the choices you make today will resonate in the strength and health of your locs tomorrow.

"There's a lot you can do with natural hair."
—*Chimamanda Ngozi Adichie*

CHAPTER THREE

Blueprint for Strong Locs

The foundation of your locs is more than just an aesthetic choice—it serves as the blueprint for their health and versatility. A well-parted foundation leads to easier loc grooming and promotes the growth of strong, uniform locs. Poorly parted foundations can lead to uneven loc sizes and sectioning, which can create visible gaps and cause challenges during loc grooming. This can also result in discomfort, scalp tension, and even contribute to hair thinning at the roots over time. The consequences of an improper foundation extend beyond appearance, affecting the overall health and maturity of your locs. As you begin your journey it's important to recognize that the foundation you establish is key to the longevity of your locs.

The essential elements needed to create your perfect foundation lie in selecting the right parting system, starting method, and loc size. In this chapter, we will explore the various hair locking and parting systems, loc sizes, and starting methods; as well as important terminology to ensure you have a thorough understanding of the fundamentals needed for strong locs.

The Role of Hair Type, Texture & Density

Before we go any further, it's important to address the misconception that only tightly coiled hair can form locs. The reality is that all hair types can cultivate locs. But if you're unfamiliar with the term hair type, let me explain.

The natural hair community often references the hair typing system popularized by hair stylist Andre Walker. This system categorizes hair into numbers (1–4) and letters (A–C). You may have seen a social media post mentioning hair types like 4A or 3C. Essentially, this hair typing system describes your curl pattern and curl depth. For instance, with a "3C" hair type, the "3" refers to a curly hair pattern, and when paired with letter "C" it represents a tighter, more densely packed curl; while "3A" would describe curly hair with a looser, more open curl depth. But as I've shared all curl patterns and hair types can successfully cultivate locs.

For that reason, it's more important to consider your hair as a whole, taking into account its texture, density, and type collectively. Understanding these characteristics about your own hair is beneficial. Especially when deciding on the type of locs you want, the size of the locs, and the ideal parting system to use when starting your loc journey.

So, what is texture? Contrary to what you may think, hair texture isn't about how your hair feels but rather the size or thickness of each individual hair strand. Regardless of your hair type, there are three basic hair textures: fine, medium, and thick.

- **Fine hair** is the most fragile texture and requires extra care to prevent breakage.

- **Medium hair** is the most common texture and is less prone to breakage compared to fine hair.

- **Thick hair** is the strongest texture and is more resistant to breakage than fine or medium hair.

The other characteristic of your hair is its **density**. Density refers to the number of hair strands per square inch on your scalp and is categorized as low, medium, or high.

- **Low-density** hair means you have fewer follicles or strands of hair per square inch on your head. Low density is also often confused with thinning, but they are not the same. For instance, you can have thick hair with low density, which may give the illusion of having a lot of hair until it is weighed down or parted, making the scalp more noticeable.

- **Medium-density** hair represents an average number of strands per square inch. This density provides the most versatility when it comes to styling, parting, and sizing locs.

- **High-density** hair means you have a substantial number of strands packed closely together. However, this high level of density can give the appearance of strong hair but actually be misleading. For example, if you have fine, high-density hair (small strands but in large quantities), you might assume your hair can handle frequent styling, but it would actually be more prone to breakage.

The importance of hair texture and density when it comes to locs becomes clear when considering the concept of the **part-to-loc ratio.** This ratio is one of the most important aspects of locs and is often emphasized by locticians. The part-to-loc ratio refers to the size of the part, or foundation of each loc, in relation to the length and weight of your hair over time.

For example, if you plan to grow your locs for 10 years and want them to reach your knees, the size of your parts will be crucial. If your foundation isn't well-balanced, by year four, your locs could begin to break due to the weight of the hair retained within each loc over the last four years.

To further illustrate, someone with **fine hair and low density** will need parts larger than someone with **fine hair and high density**. This is because lower-density hair is more likely to show scalp and may experience breakage over time as the locs grow longer and heavier.

So, understanding your hair texture and density is far more important than whether your hair type is "3B" or "4C." This knowledge of your hair will guide you in selecting the best starting method and loc size to support your hair goals. It will also help you avoid issues like breakage, thinning, and scalpiness throughout your loc journey.

Hair Locking Systems

There are three locking systems to consider when starting locs. These options include:

1. Traditional Locs

2. Microlocs

3. Freeform Locs

When considering what type of hair locking system to choose, it's very important to understand the characteristics of each option, and how each hair locking system could impact your experience.

Traditional Locs

Traditional locs are the most common type of hair locking system that you will see in the loc community. Traditional locs come in a variety of sizes, and they are one of the easiest types of locs for you to self-maintain or have a professional to maintain.

Microlocs

Microlocs are a smaller version of traditional locs. And due to their smaller size, microlocs offer greater versatility for styling compared to traditional locs or freeform locs. However, their size also requires a stricter grooming regimen to prevent thinning. As a result, maintaining microlocs is more time-consuming than other hair locking systems.

Freeform Locs

Lastly, there are **freeform locs**, or **organic locs**. With freeform locs, you essentially don't have to do anything with your hair except allow it to lock up on its own. Freeform locs will have their own unique character, and form their own unique shape throughout the loc journey. And because they are freeform, no one will have locs like yours. The outcome of freeform locs is impacted only by your hair texture, your lifestyle, and your hair care regimen.

Selecting the Best Loc Size

More often than not, locs are classified by their size more so than their hair locking system or starting method. For reference, the size chart included shows the various sizes of the locs and the classification for that size range.

Microlocs
≤ 0.3 - 0.4 cm

Pencil-Width Locs
0.5 - 0.6 cm

Thick Locs
> 1 cm

Loc Size Comparison Chart

When you start to think about the size of locs that will be best for you there are two important considerations you should have in mind:

1. **time** commitment

2. styling **versatility**

Time is one of the most precious assets we have, so be clear about the level of **time commitment** you can dedicate to your hair care from the start. If you're aiming for a low-maintenance approach with minimal time and effort invested in hair care, larger locs might be the better choice. On the other hand, if you don't mind spending hours grooming your locs at home or can visit the salon regularly for appointments, microlocs could be an ideal fit for you.

The size of your locs will play a significant role in determining what styling **versatility** your locs can accommodate. You will want to consider if you would like to experiment with the latest hairstyling trends. Choosing locs that are too thick might limit your ability to achieve certain styles, while locs that are too tiny could be prone to breakage from excessive styling. I want to assure you that, regardless of the size locs you choose, there are styles appropriate for every stage of your loc journey and every hair locking system.

Now let's go deeper and explore the loc sizes within each hair locking system to help you make a more informed decision on choosing the best size.

Sizes of Traditional Locs

What makes traditional locs one of the most popular hair locking systems is its inherent adaptability, showcased across a spectrum of sizes. The most common size within this hair locking system is often compared to the average width of a pencil, thus "pencil-width" has become synonymous with traditional-sized locs. Anything larger than pencil-width is typically classified as "medium" or "thick" locs.

Pencil-Width Locs

Pencil-Width Sized Locs

The time commitment for installation of pencil-width locs can average 2 to 4 hours when professionally installed. But when it comes to the time commitment required for grooming pencil-width locs, it varies depending on your hair texture and density. For instance, someone with medium hair texture and medium density may end up with around 70 locs, while someone with medium hair texture and high-density might have upwards of 130 locs. This spectrum of pencil-width loc sizing can result in an average at-home grooming time of 2 to 4 hours; while professional grooming averages 1 to 2 hours. And the recommended dryer time is 45 to 60 minutes on medium to high heat.

In terms of styling versatility, pencil-width locs allow for virtually all styling options. You can set them on rollers, braid them, twist them, or pin them into an elegant updo with minimal fuss.

Thick / Medium Locs

The size of thicker locs can range from "highlighter-width" to as large as your thumb. On average, you may have anywhere from 20 to 60 locs, depending on your hair texture and density.

Thick / Medium Sized Locs

One of the benefits of thicker locs is the reduced time spent on grooming, as there are fewer locs to manipulate. The average DIY grooming time is 1 to 2 hours; or 30 to 90 minutes professionally. However, this shortened grooming time is offset with longer drying time, relative to smaller locs. Because it's crucial that thicker locs are fully dried inside and out to prevent mildew growth.

When it comes to styling versatility, thicker locs can create a wide range of styles; however, some intricate styles that work well with smaller locs might not be as achievable with thicker locs.

Sizes of Microlocs

Microlocs

Microlocs range in size from slightly smaller than traditional locs to just a bit wider than a strand of thread. Their small size provides a wide variety of styling options, including roller sets, intricate updos, flat ironing, and braid or twist-outs. However, it's important to note that extension styles, such as Marley Twists or Box Braids, are not recommended for microlocs. This restriction may limit styling options for those who wish to incorporate trendy loose natural hairstyles into their loc journey.

While the small size of microlocs opens up many styling possibilities, the limitations around adding extensions may prompt some to explore alternative techniques or systems. As such various specializations of microlocs have emerged, each with its own guidelines, restrictions, and credentialing for installation and care. These variations of microlocs include well-known names like Sisterlocks™, as well as newer ones like Belle Microlocs™ and Tiny Locs™. While these systems differ in their approaches, they all produce small loc sizes, ranging from 250 to 400 locs on average.

With that being said, microlocs require an increased time commitment as compared to traditional locs. Professionally installing microlocs on 6 inches of hair can take anywhere from 8 to 12 hours, with grooming sessions averaging 3 to 4 hours every 6 weeks. Self-installation of microlocs can take 20 or more hours spread over several days, and DIY grooming may require 4 or more hours across multiple days, depending on your dexterity, and loc size. While the time investment is significant, the benefits include greater styling flexibility and prolonged neatness.

Sizes of Freeform Locs

Freeform locs, which are formed naturally as your hair grows without manipulation, create locs of various sizes. Essentially, all you need to do is care for your hair, and growth takes care of the rest. Freeform locs require minimal time commitment and offer a great deal of fullness due to the puffiness of the roots and the untamed nature of the locs themselves. However, freeform locs can often develop a flattened appearance rather than a cylindrical shape, which may slightly reduce the overall fullness. Also, when it comes to styling versatility, freeform locs are somewhat limited. The absence of defined parts and the varying sizes and shapes of the locs can make many styles difficult to achieve.

Ultimately, choosing the right loc size involves carefully considering your time commitment and desired styling versatility. After deciding on the loc size that best fits your goals, the next step is selecting a parting system to lay the foundation for your locs.

———————————————— ⊗◯●◯⊗ ————————————————

Overview of Parting Systems

A **parting system** is defined as a systematic approach to sectioning the hair. There are three commonly used parting systems for locs, each with its own advantages and disadvantages. However, before we discuss each parting system, you should understand why choosing the right one is so important— *most people overlook this crucial consideration.*

Why Parting Systems Matter

The first and most obvious reason why parting systems are important is because they serve as the **foundation for your locs**. And once the parting system is established, it cannot be changed without starting over. *Trust me—I've tried!* Changing your parting system would require either cutting your locs off or combing them out to restart your loc journey again.

The second reason why your parting system matters is because it **determines how your locs will fall.** An improperly executed parting system can significantly affect the overall look of your locs. For instance, imagine someone with high-density and thick textured hair, as their locs mature the parting system would make the difference between a beautiful, flowing silhouette and an overwhelming mop-like appearance. Which is another way to say that the parting system will determine the movement of your locs. You want your locs to flow freely and naturally, but if the parting system isn't done correctly, your locs will simply "sit" on your head.

Another important role of the parting system is to **determine how much scalp is visible**. Intentionally parting your starter locs can help offset areas with fine hair textures or low-density areas, reducing the amount of scalp that shows. Complaints about "too much scalp showing" or locs appearing "too scalpy" after grooming are often the result of an inappropriate parting system for the individual's hair type, hair texture and density. Conversely, individuals with high-density hair may prefer to choose parting systems that avoid their locs appearing overly bulky or "mop-like." The takeaway here is that the fullness you desire is largely determined by the parting system you choose.

Lastly, having a parting system makes it **easier to combine your locs** if you ever experience thinning. Without a defined parting system, blending locs together can result in uneven or awkward sections. A properly executed parting system, on the other hand, provides a systematic approach to combining locs, resulting in more consistent sizing and overall appearance.

Types of Parting Systems for Locs

The three most commonly used parting systems for starting locs are the **brick-lay parting system**, **crescent parting system**, and **diamond parting system**.

Brick-Lay Parting System

Brick-Lay Parting System for Traditional Locs

The **brick-lay parting system,** also known as square parting, is one of the most well-known ways to section your hair to start locs. *And it's really easy to do!* This parting system can be installed by a salon professional or by yourself if you choose to start your own locs. However, in either instance, you do have to be cautious of how the squares are placed on your head. If the square sections are arranged so that each row aligns directly on top of the one below it, this will create straight lines for styling purposes. However, a significant amount of scalp may be visible when the hair is not styled, especially if you have a fine hair texture, low density areas, or thicker locs.

Crescent Parting System

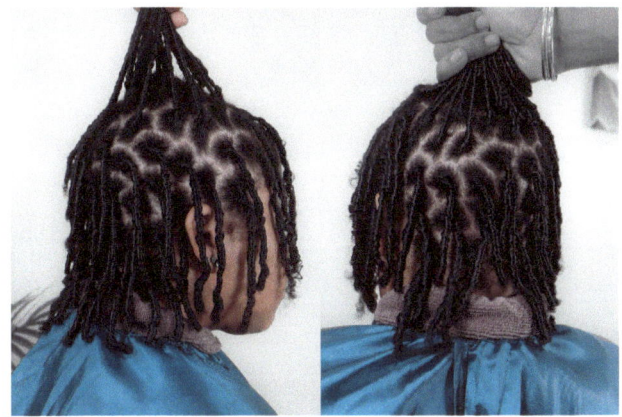

Crescent Parting System for Traditional Locs

The **crescent parting system**, also known as the c-shaped or half-moon parting, is most commonly used by those seeking a more natural or unstructured parting in their scalp. One of the key benefits of the crescent parting system is its simplicity—being that it's relatively easy to create. Additionally, this parting system provides a natural fall and face-framing effect to the locs.

Diamond Parting System

Diamond Parting System for Thick Locs and Microlocs

The **diamond parting system** is an advanced parting system because it involves creating diamond-shaped sections on a rounded surface (your head). This parting system should be executed by a professional and is not recommended as a DIY method. There are several advantages to using the diamond parting system for all sizes of locs.

One of the benefits of using a diamond parting system is that even when your hair is pulled back in a simple ponytail it appears very intricate. This makes the diamond parting system a great option if you do not like to spend a lot of time with complicated styles and prefer to wear ponytails or have your hair hang naturally. Additionally, for thicker locs or fine hair textures, the diamond parting system minimizes the visibility of the scalp. At the same time, make note that because thicker locs result in fewer individual locs, the intricate design of the diamond parting system may be less pronounced than it would be with smaller locs.

Once you've determined the parting system that you desire, the next step is selecting the installation method that will be used for starting your locs.

Starting Methods for Locs

Locs can be started naturally, instantaneously, or with extensions. The three major factors in determining the ideal method for starting your locs are: your hair texture, the length of your hair, and your skill level (or that of your chosen loctician). It's important not to start your locs with a method that doesn't align with your hair texture, length, or skill level, as it may not produce your desired aesthetic as the locs mature.

To help determine which method is best for you, we are going to explore each starting method, the advantages and disadvantages of each, and how they relate to your hair texture, length, and skill level.

Coils

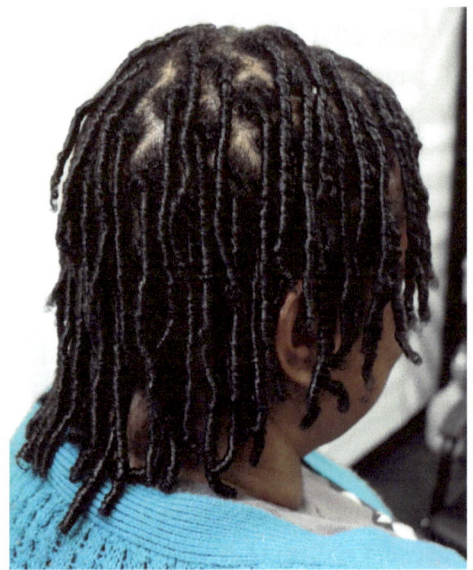

Coils As Starter Locs

The first method we will discuss is **coils.** You may also hear coils referred to as **comb coils, finger coils, or gel twists.** This is one of the most common methods for starting locs and involves using either a comb or your fingers to shape each section of hair into a cylindrical structure. Coils can be used for microlocs, traditional locs, or thick locs; however, the coil method is most effective if you have less than 6 inches of hair.

In terms of length, some locticians may start locs with coils on hair longer than 6 inches. But, the longer your hair is to start, the longer it will take for the coils to mature. You will also experience more shrinkage with coils compared to other methods because the newly formed starter locs need to tangle internally before they can begin to grow in length.

The advantage of starting locs with coils is that they are relatively easy to install and almost immediately resemble locs after installation. The disadvantage to starting locs with coils is that coils are more sensitive to water so you wouldn't be able to shampoo your hair easily or get your hair wet as often as you could with other starter loc methods.

To start locs with comb coils, you only need about 2 to 6 inches of hair (depending on your desired loc size). For microlocs, 2 inches is enough to start locs with coils, while thicker locs started with comb coils are best done on hair that is at least 5 inches.

What To Expect When Starting Locs With Coils:

Comb coils can be sensitive to water with looser curl patterns so you want to be mindful to only saturate them when you're shampooing to prevent them from coming undone. However, once the locs have entered the teenage stage, which we will discuss in the next chapter, you will no longer have to worry about unraveling. Also, since this method is created by coiling the hair in a cylindrical shape, it tends to "look like locs" faster than other methods.

Twists

Twists As Starter Locs

Twists can also be referred to as **two-strand twists, three-strand twists, or rope twists.** While twists can be done on any hair texture, they are best suited for medium to thick textures. This method is ideal if you desire thick locs, but you can also use twists to start microlocs or pencil-width traditional locs.

One downside to starting locs with twists is that the lines from the twists can take 6+ months to disappear. However, the lines will eventually fade, despite how they may look in the beginning. As long as the newly formed locs are groomed from root to ends. Another drawback is that twists can unravel during the early stages, depending on your hair texture, products you are using to groom and moisturize your locs, and your shampooing technique.

Despite the drawbacks, starting locs with twists has several advantages. First, twists provide a strong internal foundation for your new locs, eliminating the hollow space that can occur when starting with coils. Additionally, twists allow you to achieve length more quickly. Unlike coils, which need to undergo internal tangling, twists let your hair's true length appear sooner.

Locs can be started using twists with a minimum of 4 inches of hair, making twists a popular choice for longer hair. One important consideration, especially if you're planning to DIY: unlike twists for temporary natural hair styling, when using twists to start locs they must be twisted in a clockwise direction for future grooming.

What To Expect When Starting Locs With Twists:

In the beginning, your twists may unravel at the ends. To minimize unraveling, prior to shampooing your hair the **band-and-bundle method** should be used. This involves grouping several locs together and securing the ends with a rubber band. However, if unraveling does occur, you can easily twist the ends back together without completely starting over. Additionally, when starting with twists it is important to always groom the starter locs from the root to the ends in order to produce the most uniform appearance once the locs have matured.

Interlocking

Interlocking For Starter Locs

The process of **interlocking** to start locs involves using a tool and/or fingers to interweave the hair within itself, creating what is known as the internal loc matrix. Interlocking is an ideal method for starting microlocs and is a great option for people with active lifestyles and who prefer longer-lasting neatness at the roots. This method is also beneficial for individuals with product allergies or those who wish to use little to no products on their locs. Interlocking can be performed on any texture of hair with a minimum of 4 inches of hair.

The main drawback of interlocking is the difficulty in maintaining it yourself. If not done properly, it can cause significant damage to your locs, including the formation of holes, thinning, or, in the worst-case scenario, hair loss. However, one major advantage of interlocking is that your hair will remain relatively neat between grooming sessions, even if you have a very active lifestyle or your scalp sweats frequently. Additionally, since your hair is locking based on the technique itself, you won't need to use locking products for grooming.

What To Expect When Starting Locs With Interlocking:

Interlocking establishes the internal structure of the loc first, allowing shed hairs to accumulate around that foundation. As the locs mature, they will swell in size before eventually shrinking down as they progress through the later stages of the hair locking process. Locs started or maintained with interlocking may feel lumpy due to the compact nature of the interlocking pattern. While frizz is still a part of the process, the interlocking technique helps control and eventually reduce the amount of frizz along the length of the locs.

Crochet

Before and After Crochet Starter Locs

Starting locs with the crochet method, popularly known as "instant locs," requires a minimum of 4 inches of hair, and uses a micro crochet hook (0.5mm to 1.0mm) to immediately tangle the hair into a locked state. It should not be confused with interlocking or loc extensions. Unlike interlocking, which involves interweaving the hair using specific patterns, the crochet method intertwines the hair to mimic the natural cultivation of locs. And unlike loc extensions, which use added hair to create locs, the crochet method is performed entirely with your natural hair at its current length. However, pre-made loc extensions can also be added to the ends of locs using this technique.

A few drawbacks of using the crochet method include the potential for blowouts or bunching in the locs if the technique is not properly executed. These issues can result in weak areas and lumps in the locs. Another disadvantage to starting locs with the crochet method is that it will drastically shorten the length of your hair. For example, if you begin with 6 inches of loose hair, your resulting locs can measure about 3 to 4 inches in length after installation.

Conversely, one of the most significant advantages of the crochet method is that it allows you to bypass the initial stages of the locking process. Essentially, you skip the first 6 to 9 months of the locking process. Also, with this method, your locs will immediately have the appearance of mature locs from the moment they are installed.

What To Expect When Starting Locs With Crochet:

The crochet method accelerates the locking process, bringing you to the teenage stage within hours rather than months. However, your locs will still need time to mature fully, similar to naturally cultivated locs. You should expect some frizz and potential unraveling, depending on the size of the crochet hook used and the effectiveness of the technique.

Loc Extensions

*Loc Extensions Created on 4
inches of Natural Hair*

There are several options for starting locs with **loc extensions**, including attaching pre-made locs, creating loc extensions directly on your head, or transplanting naturally grown locs from another person. To start with loc extensions, you need a minimum of 3 inches of hair and you must ensure that the hair used from the loc extensions is made from natural human hair—not synthetic hair. Loc extensions can be installed on any hair texture and can be created in a variety of sizes, except for extremely small sizes of microlocs.

There are a few drawbacks to beginning your loc journey with extensions. If they are not installed properly the extensions may continuously fall out. Additionally, if synthetic hair fibers are used instead of human hair, you risk breakage and thinning of your natural hair due to the added weight of the synthetic hair. Also, color options for loc extensions can be limiting. For example, if you choose black loc extensions, even though they are made from human hair, the cleaning process used on the hair may prevent it from being dyed in the future.

Another potential drawback is that you might feel less connected to others in the loc'd community who have grown their locs naturally. While some may say you "cheated" and "skipped the awkward stage," I believe starting with loc extensions may add a layer of complexity to your loc journey. You will be challenged much sooner than someone who cultivated their locs naturally to confront the stereotypes surrounding locs. Also, in the early stages of your journey you may be forced to reflect on how your past hair choices may have aligned with societal norms rather than your personal truth.

On the other hand, there are clear advantages to starting your loc journey with extensions. For one, you will have locs instantly without waiting for your hair to lock— saving you years of time. Also, you will immediately enjoy length for styling and the versatility that comes with longer locs.

What To Expect When Starting Locs With Loc Extensions:

Loc Extensions allow you to skip the initial locking process, and instantly provides length for styling versatility. However, your root area and new growth will still need to grow through the locking process as your locs continue to mature.

Braids

Starting locs with **braids** is also known as **braid locs**. This starting method is useful if you desire microlocs or pencil-width traditional locs, and you have at least 5 inches of hair. If you have fine hair texture, an active lifestyle, or if you sweat a lot in your scalp, braids would be an ideal option for starting your locs.

One of the drawbacks of starting locs with braids is the visible lines in the starter locs. Unlike twists, however, the lines from the braids can take 12 months or more to disappear; but if you're starting with hair longer than 6 inches they may never fully disappear. Additionally, braids tend to create a linear shape, which can result in locs that are flat in appearance rather than the common cylindrical shape.

What To Expect When Starting Locs With Braids:

In the beginning, your braids may unravel at the ends. To minimize unraveling, prior to shampooing your hair the **band-and-bundle method** should be used. This involves grouping several locs together and securing the ends with a rubber band. Additionally, you can correct any unraveling by re-braiding the loose ends. It is also important to note that locs started with braids should use interlocking for grooming.

Freeform Locs

Freeform, or organic locs, are created by allowing the hair to naturally tangle on its own to form locs. Some people choose to kickstart their freeform locs using a towel or a curl sponge but that is not required. You can start freeform locs on any hair length or texture, and because the process is entirely natural, the sizes of your locs will vary.

A few drawbacks to a freeform loc journey is that you may have limited styling options because you don't have a parting system and your locs will vary in size. Also, you don't know how your locs will turn out so there's a little bit of unpredictability that may or may not be a disadvantage to you.

What To Expect When Starting Locs Freeform:

One of the biggest advantages of freeform locs is their uniqueness. No one else will have locs like yours because they reflect your hair's own natural ability to grow. Freeform locs also offer a sense of ease—there's minimal grooming, little need for products, and less concern about others' opinions since you're embracing your hair's natural locking process.

As you determine your foundation, it's important to focus on how you want your locs to look in the future, rather than what you want them to look like right now. Start by identifying the size locs you desire, then weigh the pros and cons of each parting system, and finally choose a starting method that works for you. Once you have these factors identified you will have the blueprint to begin your loc journey.

"One thing is for certain: we have always and will continue to look for meaning in our hair."
—Unknown

CHAPTER FOUR

The Beauty of the Journey

"How long will it take for my hair to lock?"

If I had a dollar for every time I've been asked this question, I'd have enough to buy every product in the ethnic hair care aisle—*at least ten times over!* But I get it. It's a valid question because patience is hard—especially when you're waiting for an unknown outcome. With my second set of locs, which I installed on my own, I found myself asking that very same question. Especially when my newly started traditional locs unraveled each time I washed them. In my desperation to stop the unraveling, I did things I would never recommend now—using tight-hold products and retwisting my locs every week. All of these efforts were in an attempt to force my hair into submission instead of letting it evolve naturally. To make it worse, as I sat under the dryer, I would scroll through social media, comparing my locs to the images I double-tapped and pinned to my inspiration board. I often questioned why my hair was so unruly and wondered what I was doing wrong.

It wasn't until I collaborated with five other content creators on a video about the biggest lessons we learn with locs that I was confronted with a truth I wasn't ready to accept. One creator shared that the biggest lesson was that **comparison is the thief of joy.** At the time, I questioned how impactful that lesson really was. I didn't get it. I compared my locs against the images on curated loc appreciation pages all the time. But as the comments and reactions to the video poured in—many viewers saying this was the message they needed most—I realized I needed to examine my own journey more closely.

It would take years for me to fully acknowledge that *this* was the most important lesson of all. I found myself reflecting on those words more and more, realizing how deeply they applied—not just to my loc journey, but to life itself. Just as I rushed through the stages of my locs, in a hurry for them to "be better," I also noticed how we often approach personal growth the same way. Oftentimes, we never pause to acknowledge how far we've come; diminishing the complex, hard work it takes to evolve. And much like personal growth, the progress doesn't begin until you stop comparing and start accepting yourself as you are in this present moment.

By the time I could look at my locs with adoration, I had already missed their true beauty. I was so focused on what my hair *wasn't* doing and how it *wasn't* looking like everyone else's on social media that I overlooked the uniqueness of its evolution. It was a tough lesson to learn, but one that deepened my appreciation for the process. Every stage has its own challenges, lessons, and opportunities to flourish, but when we rush through them, we rob ourselves of the experience. I emphasize this because as you begin your loc journey, I encourage you to focus on the beauty of the journey—not just the destination. My hope is that this chapter helps you understand what to expect in each stage of the hair locking process so you can appreciate where you are and where you're growing.

The Stages of Hair Locking

Essentially there are four main stages of the hair locking process: the starter loc stage, the baby loc stage, the teenage stage, and the adult stage. However, a fifth stage—the elder stage—is reached when locs have matured for five or more years. During this stage, locs often experience a natural shedding process before returning to the adult stage. So while most of the transformation occurs during the starter through teenage stages, the adult stage is the longest.

On average, moving through the first four stages takes an average of **9 to 18 months**. However, factors such as your hair texture, hair density, product usage, and your daily hair care regimen can cause your locs to progress faster or slower through the stages of hair locking.

Understanding the unique characteristics of each stage is essential in recognizing where your locs are in their evolution. Throughout this chapter, you'll see photos of the same set of locs to illustrate how hair transforms across each stage of the locking process—from the beginning to maturity.

So, let's explore each stage in detail.

Starter Loc Stage

Starter Locs with Twists

Characteristics of Starter Locs:

- Small in diameter

- Clean parts

- Puffiness at the roots

In the **starter loc stage**, you establish your locs using your chosen parting system and starting method. Essentially, this stage lays the foundation for how your hair will tangle onto and within itself to begin forming locs. So, from the moment you leave the salon with your new locs or finish parting and forming your own foundation at home you are officially in the starter loc stage!

However, people around you might see this stage as a temporary style change rather than a committed step in the process of hair locking. For that reason, this stage is often mistaken as just another hairstyle. It's not unusual for those used to seeing you with your loose hair to be puzzled by your new foundation. Therefore, it's important to anticipate and be ready for questions, curious glances, and the occasional disapproving expression— *it's all part of the journey.*

During this stage, you're waiting for your hair to begin tangling, as known as **budding**. This refers to the formation and accumulation of tangled hair within the loc shaft. But if you were unsure of what it means when your locs start "budding", you'll likely feel more concern than excitement when it happens. Common questions at this stage include: *"Why does my loc look pregnant?"* and *"What is this lump in my locs?"* It's completely normal to think something is "wrong"— *but don't worry!* Subtle tangling is happening each time you moisturize or cleanse your hair that helps your hair to begin transforming into mature locs. On average, it takes **3 to 6 months** for your entire head to progress to the next stage.

Additionally, during the starter loc stage, grooming sessions tend to take longer and require extra attention to detail. Each loc should be carefully examined for signs of unraveling and intentionally maintained to support its evolution to the next stage.

If your locs haven't begun budding within the first six months, check your products first. Without the guidance of a certified loctician, many people unknowingly use products that slow down the locking process. However, keep in mind that the timeline for budding varies from person to person and across different hair textures, so patience is required.

My Experience With The Starter Loc Stage:

To begin my third set of locs, I chose to start with twists. As a result of my naturally curly hair, my head resembled a ball of frizz after the first shampoo. While I cared little about my family's opinions—knowing they wouldn't understand anyway—anxiety showed up when it came to social gatherings and corporate events. As I struggled with my self-esteem, an internal dialogue persisted: *I can't go out in public with my hair looking like this.*

My reaction was rooted in shame. I often stood in front of the mirror, attempting to style my starter locs into something deemed "presentable." But I would often resort to headwraps or headbands to conceal the frizz. However, one day, I reached a breaking point. I was tired of feeling judged and criticized. I made a decision: *This is my hair. Take it or leave it.*

It was only after I reminded myself that *I was enough* that I began to notice the people staring in awe—not in disapproval. The more I affirmed myself, the more affirmation I received from others. It was as if a light switch had been flipped, illuminating the beauty that had always been there.

Baby Loc Stage

Buds Forming in Locs

Characteristics of Baby Locs:

- Frizzy

- Budding

- Swelling in size

Once the majority of your hair has begun to bud, you will enter the **baby locs stage.** This is an exciting milestone in your loc journey—budding means your hair is beginning to lock!

In this stage, your hair will be noticeably frizzy and swollen. To support the locking process, it's essential to keep your hair clean and maintain a regular cleansing and grooming routine. This helps prevent buildup and encourages uniform locking throughout your locs. It's also important to limit styling during this stage. Excessive styling can disrupt the uniformity of your locs and may slow down, or even prevent them from fully budding. However, if you must style your locs, opt for styles like pin curls or roller sets, as they allow the hair to lock without excessive compression. Also, before styling make sure your hair is completely dry—styling wet baby locs can negatively interfere with the locking process.

On average, you can expect to be in the baby locs stage between **3 to 9 months**; although it can take longer. The duration depends on factors like hair type and length. Longer hair typically takes more time to fully lock, as it must go through the natural process of tangling and shrinking. For example, if you start locs with shoulder-length hair, your locs may still be at—or even shorter than—shoulder length a year later. On the other hand, shorter hair tends to bud faster and retain length more quickly since there's less hair that needs to tangle.

When it comes to how hair type affects the locking process, looser curl patterns tend to take longer to lock, as compared to tighter curl patterns. It's also common to have multiple curl patterns throughout your hair, which means some areas may lock more quickly than others.

Teenage Stage

Traditional Locs in Teenage Stage

Characteristics of Teenage Locs:

- Double Original Width

- Wild

- Shrinkage

After your hair has fully budded along the entire length of your locs and swelled to nearly twice its original size, you have entered the **teenage stage**. You may have heard this stage referred to as the "ugly phase" or "awkward stage." These negative labels typically come from the common characteristics of this phase, including unruly hair, excessive frizz, and shrinkage.

At this stage, many people misinterpret their hair as fully locked because the most significant changes are happening internally rather than externally. The complex matting and intertwining that occurs often cause the locs to feel harder and more dense. As a result, some people make the mistake of using softening products, such as cream conditioners, in an attempt to make their locs feel softer like in previous stages. However, overusing softening products can cause weakness and even reverse the progress made thus far in the locking process.

You also want to consider the impact of styling your locs at this stage. The recommended styles for this stage are "compression styles," such as rope twists and braids, because they help manage swelling and encourage the locs to condense more quickly. However, frequent styling can lead to lumps and inconsistencies in your locs, so less is more.

On average, the teenage stage lasts anywhere from **6 to 18 months**. Once the external frizz has settled into the locs and their size has compacted, you'll notice that your locs feel more solid and structured. These changes are evidence that your locs are transitioning into the adult stage.

Adult Stage

Traditional Locs in the Adult Stage

Characteristics of Adult Locs:

- Dense

- Sealed Ends

- Length Retention

- Minimal / No Frizz

When you've reached the **adult stage**, your locs will have become dense, and you will start to notice more length retention. The size of your locs will also have normalized— after initially being skinny, then swelling to nearly twice their size, they will now remain consistently compacted.

In the adult stage, grooming sessions are shorter since there is little to no frizz along the shaft. Additionally, now that your locs have fully matured, you can style them when your hair is wet or dry without the risk of creating lumps or weakness.

Your locs will remain in this stage the longest—on average, about 5 years—before transitioning into the elder stage of the locking process. However, reaching the adult stage can take anywhere from **12 to 36 months**, depending on factors such as hair texture, hair length, grooming routine, and overall hair care.

Elder Stage

Tip Separating From End of a Loc

Characteristics of Elder Locs:

- Loose Ends

- Tip Separation

The elder stage is one of the least discussed stages of the locking process. During this stage, the ends of the locs begin to atrophy, or deteriorate.

When your locs reach the **elder stage**, you may notice that the tips, or the last 1 to 3 inches of your locs, start to weaken or soften; a process similar to split ends in loose natural hair.

To prevent excessive breakage or uneven separation, it is advised that you trim your locs approximately every five years. This helps promote stronger locs and maintains healthier ends. However, if you prefer not to trim, you can allow the ends to naturally separate over time. Once the tips shed, your locs will return back to the adult stage.

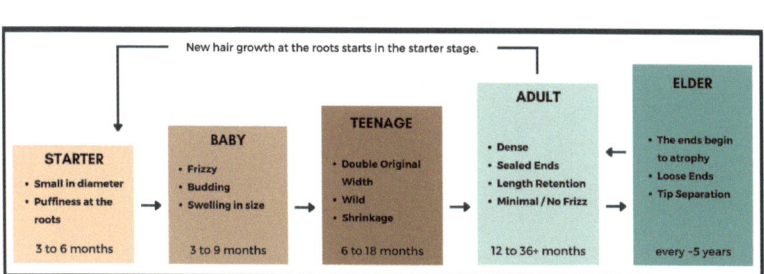

Stages of Hair Locking

The hair locking process is a continuous journey that can span months to years of cultivation. What's important for you to remember is that your hair is always evolving. At any given moment, different sections of your locs may be in different stages—your ends, the oldest part, may have reached the adult stage, while the middle is still in the teenage phase, and your roots are just beginning the baby loc stage. This natural evolution is part of the beauty of the process. So, don't be discouraged if your locs don't look mature right away. Everyone's timeline is different, but the destination is the same—beautifully cultivated locs.

As you continue on your loc journey, maintaining the health and strength of your locs becomes just as important as their growth. In the next chapter, we'll explore loc grooming—the process of shaping and nurturing your locs for lasting health and beauty.

"Never regret your mistakes. Admire the courage it took to attempt the unknown."
—Unknown

CHAPTER FIVE

Healthy Loc Grooming

A year after graduating college, I began my first loc journey with Sisterlocks™, which use the interlocking technique for starting and grooming locs. During the 26-hour installation, I experienced slight discomfort as small sections of my hair were woven into over 300 locs. This discomfort was familiar—it reminded me of the tightness I had felt as a child getting box braids. However, my excitement far outweighed any pain. I looked forward to the freedom interlocking would provide: exercising without worry, weekly shampooing, and versatile hairstyling. Plus, the assurance that my soft, frizzy hair would remain tamed and secure made the process feel worthwhile.

But as the weeks passed, the mandatory retightening sessions every six weeks became a painful reality check. Since I was no longer detangling my hair every week, my scalp had grown unfamiliar with manipulation, making each retightening session intensely painful. The soreness echoed memories of my childhood experiences with relaxed hair, serving as an intense reminder of the abusive self-care practices I had intended to leave behind. Unfortunately, it wasn't until years later—after removing the Sisterlocks™ and restarting with traditional locs—that I realized interlocking wasn't the right fit for me at the time.

I share this realization with you because understanding the various loc grooming methods isn't just about aesthetics; it's a necessary part of nurturing your crown. While each method produces different aesthetic results, they all serve the same purpose—to shape and groom your locs as they mature. And understanding the differences between these techniques, along with the tools and products required, will empower you to choose a method that best aligns with your hair type, lifestyle, and hair locking system. In this chapter, we will also dispel common myths about maintaining your locs that often lead to unnecessary damage or confusion when misunderstood.

Loc Grooming Techniques

There are three primary grooming techniques for locs: hand grooming, interlocking, and crochet.

Hand-Grooming

Hand grooming can be performed using either **palm-rolling** or **loc smything**. These methods are commonly referred to as **retwisting.** While the methods for retwisting are similar in purpose they each have benefits that make them unique.

Palm-Rolling

This is one of the most widely recognized techniques for grooming locs. With palm-rolling, you use either your hands (palms) or a comb to groom the new growth of your locs.

The purpose of palm-rolling is to use the palms of your hands to manipulate loose hairs into a cylindrical shape, guiding them into the shaft of the locs before securing each loc with clips. A hooded hair dryer is then used to set the hair in place. Essentially, with palm-rolling, the hair is "doing the work" of locking itself over time.

This grooming technique is mainly used for traditional locs, but it can also be used on microlocs. In this case, it is recommended no more than once every 3 to 4 weeks. A retwist grooming session is typically completed within 2 to 4 hours at home, depending on your speed and dexterity.

Advantages of Palm-Rolling

- **Time-Saving.** On average, a loctician can complete your palm-roll grooming within 1 to 2 hours, whereas interlocking or crochet grooming sessions can take upwards of 3 to 4 hours when professionally done.

- **Simple.** By using your hands to cultivate the locs, palm-roll grooming is simple enough to be done at home.

Disadvantages of Palm Rolling

- **Over manipulation.** If palm-rolling is done too frequently or too tightly, it can lead to significant thinning or even hair loss—known as traction alopecia—all in an attempt to keep your locs "neat."

- **Unraveling**. One of the biggest complaints about palm-rolling is that it does not last for a long time and the hair at the roots begins to unravel or frizz within a few days.

Using A Comb to Retwist Locs

A comb is used for locs shorter than 4 inches in length, while retwisting by hand is recommended for locs longer than 4 inches. Using the palms of your hands will give your locs a more natural appearance; whereas retwisting with a comb results in a neater look—*but at a cost.*

Essentially, a comb detangles the hair at the roots before reshaping it. This matters because locs form through the natural tangling of hair. If your hair is already intertwining at the root as it grows out and you use your hands to shape it, you accelerate the locking process. However, when using a comb, it first untangles the hair, forcing it to go through the tangling process again before it can begin locking.

The use of a comb for retwisting is more in alignment with a stylistic approach to hair locking because it prioritizes a neat, uniform appearance over the natural cultivation of the hair.

While using a comb may not be the most ideal approach for a holistic approach to grooming, there is a hand-grooming technique that minimizes frizz, extends the longevity of the retwist, and creates neatness without a comb—this technique is known as **Loc Smything**.

Loc Smything

Master Pioneer Ona Osirio-Maat coined the hand grooming technique known as **Loc Smything** in 1989. Osirio-Maat studied the hand positioning of Ancient Egyptians to uncover how locs were groomed for kings and queens. Her discoveries led her to develop and teach the Loc Smything technique.

This hand grooming method provides greater control of loose hairs and offers a longer-lasting hold without the necessity of locking products.

While it is similar to palm-rolling in that the hair gradually locks over time, one key difference is how the locs are formed.

With Loc Smything, loose hairs are uniformly wrapped around the shaft of the loc multiple times to create a solid, cylindrical shape. Because of the uniform wrapping this technique is especially beneficial for those with fine, wavy, or curly hair, as it helps control the frizz.

Advantages of Loc Smything

- **Longer Lasting Hold.** Unlike palm-rolling, which wraps loose hair around the loc once and relies on clips to secure it in place, Loc Smything wraps the loose hair around the loc shaft multiple times, creating a stronger, longer-lasting hold.

- **No Product Needed.** This technique allows for a minimalist approach to hair care, giving you a lighter feel to your locs and reduces the risk of product buildup.

Disadvantages of Loc Smything

- **Difficult Learning Curve.** While some may find Loc Smything intuitive, for the majority, this technique initially feels awkward and requires patience and practice to master—especially when grooming your own locs at home.

- **Size Limitations**. Loc Smything works best for traditional locs. When used on smaller locs, such as microlocs, the hand positioning and motion can be challenging. While this technique can help to control frizz in smaller locs, it is not recommended for frequent usage.

Interlocking

Interlocking is most commonly known for its use in the microlocs hair locking system. This grooming technique, which is also referred to as **retightening,** involves pulling the end of the loc through the root to control new growth at the scalp. It can be performed using a specialized tool or with your fingers. For fine hair textures or individuals with an active lifestyle interlocking is the ideal grooming method. When self-grooming, a retightening session on microlocs, can take anywhere from 6 to 8 hours, depending on your skill level and dexterity.

Advantages of Interlocking

- **Longer-Lasting Results.** The time between each grooming session is significantly longer when maintaining your locs with interlocking than with hand grooming. On average, interlocked locs are groomed every 6 to 8 weeks, whereas palm-rolled locs typically require maintenance once a month.

- **Suitable For All Hair Types.** The interlocking technique minimizes unraveling and keeps the hair bound throughout the locking process, even with regular shampooing and sweating.

Disadvantages of Interlocking

- **Smaller Locs.** Interlocking is best suited for smaller locs, making it rare to see thick locs maintained with this method.

- **Potentially Damaging.** Interlocking requires the use of specific rotational patterns, and when not performed correctly, can result in holes forming within the locs that lead to breakage and/or thinning. Also, uneven tension during grooming can cause thinning at the roots or even trigger hair loss, also known as traction alopecia. Therefore, a level of training is advised before attempting interlocking at home.

You may also hear criticisms surrounding the interlocking technique causing thinning locs, lumps, or hair breakage. While these issues can occur with interlocked locs, they are not often caused by interlocking itself but rather by improper technique and the use of incorrect tools.

Choosing The Right Tool for Interlocking

To ensure consistent tension when interlocking, I highly recommend using a tool specifically designed for this technique. The tool should be **gentle on the hair**, **appropriately sized** for your locs, and **effective at controlling the surrounding hair** during the grooming process. Additionally, it **should not snag** or cause unnecessary stress on your locs while grooming. Below are a few of the commonly used tools for interlocking:

Nappylocs Tool

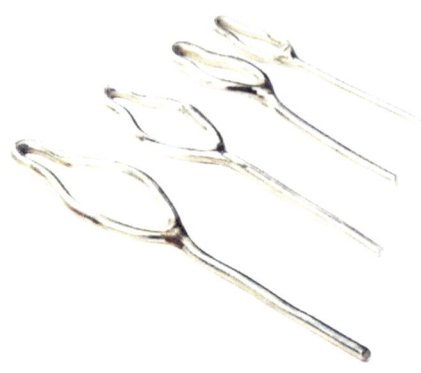

The nappylocs tool by *Nappy N Happy* is specifically designed for interlocking locs and works well on locs of all sizes. However, because each loc needs to be individually threaded through the tool, self-grooming can become very time consuming.

Advantages:

• Designed for locs
• Will not snag hair
• Comes in various sizes

Disadvantages:

• Bends easily, requiring reshaping
• Time consuming grooming sessions
• Easy to lose

Dual Interlocking Tool

The dual interlocking tool combines two tools, one for interlocking microlocs and the other for traditional locs. This adaptable design makes it the most cost-effective and efficient tool for interlocking locs of all sizes.

Advantages:

- Works for all sizes of locs
- Will not damage hair
- Designed for interlocking

Disadvantages:

- Takes practice to hold/use

When using the proper tool for interlocking, you will not only save yourself time, but also help ensure your locs remain strong. It is inevitable that new tools for interlocking will be created over time. I encourage you to evaluate any tools using this criteria: the tool should be gentle on the hair, appropriately sized for your locs, effective at controlling the surrounding hair during the grooming process, and it should not snag or cause unnecessary stress on your locs while grooming. For more information and training on interlocking techniques, enroll in online classes at educationforlocs.com.

Crochet Grooming

Crochet Grooming on Traditional Locs

Crochet grooming for locs is a meticulous technique that uses a micro crochet hook to replicate the natural tangling of the hair as it grows into locs. This technique is most effective at controlling loose hairs along the shaft of the locs, while also providing a neat appearance and fullness at the roots. The versatility of crochet grooming is also highlighted in its ability to cater to all hair types, especially straight and wavy hair. However, this grooming technique is best used on traditional locs and is not recommended for microlocs. When self grooming, it can take an average of 3 to 4 hours to complete a crochet grooming session on traditional locs depending on your skill level and dexterity.

Advantages of Crochet Grooming

- **Controls Frizz.** Crochet grooming allows you to reduce and nearly eliminate frizz, creating neat, frizz-free locs.

- **Fullness At The Roots.** This technique is especially beneficial for fine hair, as crochet grooming adds volume at the roots, and avoids the flat appearance that often results from palm-rolling or interlocking.

Disadvantages of Crochet Grooming

- **Must Use A Specialty Tool.** A micro crochet hook (0.50mm or less) is the ideal tool for crochet grooming. When larger crochet hooks are used they damage hairs inside of the locs and over time can result in areas of weakness.

- **Uncomfortable.** Keep in mind that crochet grooming mimics the natural matting process by weaving and tangling hair strands together. For those who are tender-headed or have a sensitive scalp, this technique can be quite uncomfortable or even painful.

Products for Loc Grooming

When it comes to products for loc grooming, my motto is **"less is more."** However, that wasn't always the case. As I shared earlier, when I began my first set of traditional locs, I used any product with the word "hold" in the name. I assumed my fine hair texture needed to be held in place or it would never lock. I religiously applied shea butter-based loc balm and extreme-hold locking gel. The result: my locs were shiny, had little to no frizz, and barely moved because they were so stiff. At this time, I had no reference to tell me this wasn't healthy or natural—especially since the products I was using featured aloe plants and people with locs on the packaging. I thought they were the *right* products to use. I believed everyone *had* to use them to start locs. *I was so wrong.* And I learned an important lesson, the hard way.

Products DO NOT lock hair. As I shared my journey on my blog, discussing the lineup of products I thought I "needed", my comment section filled with disapproving messages from members of the freeform loc community. They urged me to think about people with freeform locs who don't retwist or use locking products, yet their hair still locks. That realization was eye-opening for me at the time. Thankfully, I didn't take their comments personally. Instead, I heeded their warnings. So, I repeat—**products DO NOT lock hair.**

Now, you may be asking yourself, *"Well, what's the point of using locking products at all?"* Allow me to explain. With a holistic approach to hair locking, the purpose of using products during grooming is to add shine, create a polished finish, and nourish the hair. Locking products should not be relied on to actually lock your hair—your hair will naturally loc on its own over time. Your grooming technique will shape your locs, while the right products will keep your hair nourished and strong.

After detoxing my stiff, frizz-free locs, I finally understood what the freeform community was trying to tell me. The basin I used for my first detox was filled with buildup—the water turned from clear to a murky brown. Afterwards, my locs had never felt so light and soft as they did once I removed all of the tight-hold gel and shea butter. I adopted the "less is more" approach, and my locs began to thrive.

With that in mind, here is a list of products that can be used for holistic loc grooming:

- **Aloe Vera Gel.** The aloe vera plant is over 95% water, and water is exactly what hair needs to tangle and mature through the locking process. Additionally, aloe vera gel provides a flexible hold to prevent locs from becoming stiff after drying. I recommend using food-grade aloe vera rather than aloe vera formulated for skin issues like sunburn, as the latter can cause flaking or leave residue in the hair.

- **Styling Foam.** It is true, you can retwist your locs using foam! Styling foam, or mousse as some people like to call it, is a lightweight liquid that helps set styles in place. When used for a retwist, it can effectively hold the shape of the grooming. However, not all foams are created equal. When selecting a foam for retwisting, ensure it is oil-free and non-sticky once it dries, to prevent buildup.

- **Water & Oil.** For a minimalist, holistic approach, you can simply apply a light oil to your locs after the cleansing process, then proceed with grooming—no additional product is necessary. This method allows your hair to mature naturally through the locking process, without relying on gels, butters, or styling foams.

While these are my recommended product choices for grooming, it's equally important to discuss what to avoid. Using products not specifically formulated for locs can be detrimental to their health, leading to scalp issues, buildup, breakage, and thinning.

Products to Avoid for Loc Grooming

Here are four types of products you should avoid—or, if you've been using them, discontinue immediately and perform a thorough loc detox:

1. **Wax.** Products that contain wax—including beeswax—are detrimental to locs over time. Wax is not water soluble meaning it will be extremely difficult to wash away, especially from within the locs. With continued usage, the wax builds up and it can make locs unnaturally heavy, leading to breakage and thinning as the hair grows longer. Additionally, wax prevents moisture from penetrating the cortex (the internal area of the hair strands where moisture is stored), resulting in dryness and brittleness.

2. **Brown Gel.** This type of gel is typically used for braiding and hard sets like fingerwaves. So while "brown gel" may provide a lasting hold, it is loaded with parabens, artificial colors, and excessive protein. The overuse of protein can actually weaken your locs, making them hard, brittle, and prone to breakage.

3. **Creams.** Cream-based products are often too thick and heavy for locs, preventing the hair from properly intertwining and locking. Thus, using these products can slow down the locking process and lead to buildup over time.

4. **Unhealthy Ingredients.** Be cautious of products with long ingredient lists full of chemicals that are difficult to pronounce. Products like this often contain harmful preservatives such as

parabens, formaldehyde, and phthalates, which can irritate your scalp and negatively affect your health. To prioritize the health of your locs it is important to read product labels thoroughly and not just focus on attractive packaging. Also, shopping with brands that genuinely care about your hair's wellbeing will give you a peace of mind.

Myths About Loc Grooming

Now, let's debunk three of the common myths surrounding loc grooming to ensure you avoid any confusion that could lead to damage.

Myth: I constantly have loose hair at the roots and my hair is not locking.

Reality: Having loose hairs at the root that aren't connected to your locs is very common— especially for those with wavy or curly hair types, or fine hair textures. This occurs because your hair grows away from your locs rather than into them. As a result, you need to incorporate two key factors into your regimen: **staying consistent with grooming** and **controlling flyaways.**

It's a misconception that everyone can go months without grooming their locs (also known as semi-freeforming) and that doing so will automatically make them thicker. If your hair naturally grows away from your locs, it is best to set a consistent grooming schedule. Ideally:

Hand-Grooming every 4 to 6 weeks

Interlocking every 6 to 9 weeks

Crocheting every 8 to 12 weeks

Sticking to a schedule that works for you helps train your hair to stay within your locs and minimizes excessive amounts of frizz. However, keep in mind that new hairs are constantly growing, so consistent grooming is necessary as long as you have locs.

Myth: A retwist should last for 4 weeks or more.

Reality: For most hair textures, a retwist, when using a holistic approach to grooming, will **last up to two weeks at best**. And by "last," I mean staying together at the roots without unraveling or loosening. However, if you ask a loctician who has a stylistic approach to hair locking, they will likely tell you that a retwist should last four or more weeks. While this is possible, the types of products required to achieve that longevity often lead to extreme buildup.

I would even challenge you to consider whether the expectation for locs to stay in place for 4+ weeks is a byproduct of European beauty standards? *Think about it*—our hair is textured. Our hair has curls, coils, kinks, and waves that do not naturally lay flat. Yet, we've been led to believe that "laid" hair is the standard, resulting in us buying "tight hold", "no frizz", and edge control products to subdue our natural texture.

I encourage you not to become frustrated with your retwist unraveling or loosening at the roots because it's a natural part of the process. Let go of the need for stiff, flat hair and embrace the process with patience. Instead of working against your hair, learn to work with it. Longer-lasting retwists aren't achieved through heavy products that suffocate your hair and scalp, but through using and practicing the right grooming technique.

Myth: Not retwisting your locs will cause them to grow thicker.

Reality: Not retwisting your locs can actually lead to thinning if your hair texture and overall hair health cannot withstand the absence of retwisting. For wavy and curly hair types, or fine hair textures, skipping regular retwisting—once per month—can actually cause damage. The culprit behind this damage is hair growing away from your locs. If left unchecked for weeks, this will lead to the roots thinning and eventually breaking.

So, instead of avoiding retwisting in hopes of achieving thicker locs, understand that if your locs aren't maturing to the desired size, the issue is a result of the foundation, or parting system, not the frequency of grooming. To truly cultivate thicker locs, restarting with appropriately sized parts based on your hair texture and density is the key. Remember, strong, thick locs are created with care, not neglect.

Hopefully, you have now gained a clear understanding of the purpose behind loc grooming techniques, as well as the tools and products they require. And you feel confident in choosing a grooming method that works for your hair type and lifestyle.

"Healthy locs grow from a healthy scalp."
—Nicole J, A Distinct Image

CHAPTER SIX

Wash Smarter, Not Harder

When it comes to Black hair care, social media has been both a gift and a curse. Before 2008, the knowledge and wisdom of how to care for textured hair were almost exclusively in the hands of professionals. Black women regularly visited salons two to four times per month for hair appointments that often lasted all day. To be a cosmetologist, natural hair stylist, or loctician was a coveted position in the community. However, the introduction of social media turned that rite of passage and community influence upside down.

Seemingly overnight, "beauty influencers" began sharing their hair care practices and product recommendations as gospel, shifting the power from salon professionals to social media personalities. You no longer needed to spend the weekend in the salon or pay a professional to do your hair—now, you just needed an internet connection in order to access hundreds of "tutorials" at your fingertips. At the same time, aspiring hair experts no longer needed formal training or a costly education. If you had a few hundred followers or thousands of views, the community trusted you. The power dynamic shifted quickly, and because the majority of salon professionals with decades of experience refused to freely share their knowledge and wisdom on social media, misinformation went viral.

Many influencers shared their trial-and-error experiences when it came to hair care for locs as best practices. It was easy to press record, share a tutorial of a new product, rave about instant results, and upload the video—without any obligation to follow up weeks later with a true evaluation of its effects. And instead of tried-and-true methods vetted by locticians who work with hundreds of clients and various hair types, the norm became ever-changing product recommendations and unsupported routines shared by everyday people. This opened the door for product companies to push low-quality products with high-impact marketing, using influencers to target people desperate for answers their stylists would no longer share without an appointment.

At a time when few, if any, locticians were posting online about loc care—let alone the journey to starting locs—beauty influencers simply repeated what they had heard, whether the information was true or not. As a result, content shared about locs was rooted in ignorance and often reinforced negative stereotypes that locs are dry, dirty, and unprofessional. You've likely seen videos of influencers slathering their hair with oil, claiming it provides moisture—despite the fact that moisture comes from water. I've personally lost count of the videos shared on how to style locs for the workplace in which the solution is to cover them with a wig or "protective style". You've probably also come across at least one video advocating against shampooing starter locs for months to "help them lock", which further perpetuates the myth that locs are formed with dirt and sweat.

However, cleanliness is essential for strong, healthy locs. Regularly shampooing your hair is necessary— especially in the beginning stages. Clean hair not only encourages hair locking but also prevents buildup, odor, and potential scalp issues. So, whether or not you see a loctician for regular grooming, you should be shampooing and conditioning your locs at home.

This chapter will help you understand the types of shampoo to use and how to properly condition your locs for long-term health.

Types of Shampoo for Locs

The primary types of shampoo that are used and recommended for locs include **clarifying, chelating, medicated,** and **moisturizing shampoo.**

Clarifying Shampoo

The purpose of clarifying shampoo is to deeply cleanse the hair, specifically removing accumulated buildup, residue, and impurities from within your locs. Without removal, this buildup can lead to dullness, stiffness, and even odor. With that in mind, it's essential to always include a clarifying shampoo in your hair care regimen. To ensure the clarifying shampoo effectively attracts and removes buildup, it is recommended to allow it to sit on your scalp and throughout your locs for 3 to 5 minutes.

Chelating Shampoo

Chelating shampoo is a type of clarifying shampoo designed to remove mineral deposits caused by hard water or chlorinated pools. These mineral deposits can leave your locs feeling stiff and looking dull, even after moisturizing. If you live in an area with hard water or you swim regularly, it is highly recommended that you use a chelating shampoo. You can identify a chelating shampoo by checking the label—it will state that it is formulated to remove mineral deposits and/or is suitable for swimmers.

Medicated Shampoo

Medicated shampoo is formulated to address scalp issues such as dandruff, scalp psoriasis, or seborrheic dermatitis. If you're experiencing scalp discomfort or flakiness, a medicated shampoo might be the solution. Over-the-counter medicated shampoos typically contain a low-dose antifungal treatment, while those prescribed by a physician may have higher concentrations for quicker results. The benefits of using medicated shampoo, particularly if you have a scalp condition, include relief from itching, irritation, and redness, as well as reduced flakiness caused by dandruff or other scalp concerns.

When using a medicated shampoo, it is very important to let it sit on the scalp —not the hair—for at least five minutes to ensure it effectively treats the condition. Typically, medicated shampoos can cause dryness in the hair. So, it is recommended to always follow up with a moisturizing shampoo or conditioning treatment.

Moisturizing Shampoo

The purpose of moisturizing shampoo is to replenish oils lost during the clarifying process and help to balance the hair's pH. It is optional to use a moisturizing shampoo as long as a medicated shampoo is not in use. However, a moisturizing shampoo is highly recommended for thicker hair textures and color-treated hair, which are more prone to dryness and damage from frequent cleansing.

While moisturizing shampoos can be beneficial for locs, using them in moderation is key. When choosing a moisturizing shampoo, it is important to choose a **sulfate-free moisturizing shampoo** to ensure the hair and scalp receive proper nourishment without stripping the hair. Overusing moisturizing shampoo can lead to buildup within the locs, causing other issues.

Finding the right balance and understanding your locs' specific moisture needs may require some trial and error if you choose to DIY. However, there are some cleansing best practices that I can share with you.

Choosing the Right Shampoo for Your Locs

The combination and type of shampoo you choose for your locs should align with your specific needs and hair type. Here are some key considerations when selecting the right shampoo(s):

Straight, Wavy or Curly Hair Types: People with straight, wavy, or curly hair may benefit from a shampoo regimen that includes using a clarifying shampoo twice, and optionally followed by a moisturizing shampoo. This approach helps promote the locking process and minimizes unraveling during the early stages. However, be mindful when using clarifying shampoo back-to-back, it is important to follow up with a conditioning treatment to maintain moisture and prevent excessive dryness in your locs.

Coily Hair: Those with tightly-coiled hair types may require more moisture, making moisturizing shampoos a necessary addition to your regimen. Following a shampoo regimen that includes a clarifying shampoo first then a moisturizing shampoo, even in the starter loc stages, can help to maintain a healthy moisture balance in the hair.

Areas With Hard Water: If you notice soap scum on your faucet or bathtub, it is an indication that you live in an area with hard water. To keep your locs from becoming brittle and appearing dull it is important to use a chelating shampoo, instead of a general clarifying shampoo. This will help to remove mineral deposits left in the hair by hard water. Following a shampoo regimen that uses a chelating shampoo one to two times before conditioning is ideal.

Scalp Condition: If you have a specific scalp condition like dandruff, scalp psoriasis, or seborrheic dermatitis, try an over the counter medicated shampoo and/or consult with a dermatologist for a prescription strength medicated shampoo. The shampoo regimen that you should follow includes a clarifying shampoo first, followed by a medicated shampoo, and ending with a moisturizing shampoo.

While it's important that you select the right type of shampoo for your needs, it's equally important not to overly cleanse your hair.

Tips for Effectively Shampooing Locs at Home

I believe it's helpful to understand the nuanced differences between caring for loose hair versus locs, especially when it comes to cleansing. Unlike individual strands of loose hair, locs are an intricate accumulation of shed and actively growing hair that create pockets where product and debris can become trapped. This unique structure makes proper cleansing essential to prevent odors, buildup, and avoid potential fungal overgrowth. So, while shampooing may have been infrequent or optional with your loose hair, it becomes a non-negotiable practice with locs.

Here are four practical tips to ensure effective shampooing at home:

1. **Always Clarify First.** Clarifying shampoo effectively removes product residues, environmental pollutants, and excess oils from the hair. Additionally, by clarifying first, you allow conditioning and moisturizing products to penetrate the hair strands more effectively, leading to healthier, more vibrant locs.

2. **Don't Wait Too Long.** Ideally, you should aim to shampoo your locs every 2 to 3 weeks, but no more than every 7 days and wait

no longer than 30 days between cleansing. Over-shampooing can strip your locs of natural oils, leading to dryness and brittleness, while infrequent shampooing can result in buildup.

3. **Water Pressure Matters.** The typical shower head or sink faucet may not produce enough water pressure to effectively loosen buildup, dirt, and oils that have settled within your locs since the last shampoo. A detachable shower head or faucet with adjustable water settings to increase the concentration of water is highly recommended to ensure a deep cleanse at home.

4. **Rinse! And Rinse Some More!** You should rinse your locs for a *minimum* of 15 minutes—or longer if your locs extend past your shoulders! Think about it: your locs are made up of compacted, intertwined hair, and you need to reach the center to fully remove any shampoo residue. To ensure you are reaching the core of your locs, always listen to your hair— *literally.* After rinsing for at least 15 minutes, run your hands through your locs. If you hear a sudsy, soap sound, rinse again!

Ultimately, a balanced approach to shampooing your locs is required. Trust your scalp and observe how your hair responds to different shampoos. Adjust your shampooing frequency and product choices based on your hair's unique needs. By following these tips, you'll ensure that your hair stays clean. *But what about your scalp?*

Scalp health is just as important for maintaining healthy locs. Let's explore how to pre-treat your scalp for the most effective cleansing experience.

Pre-Treatment for Locs

A **pre-treatment**, or pre-cleanse, for locs typically involves applying a specialized product or shampoo to the scalp before the regular cleansing process. The purpose of the pre-treatment is to help dissolve oils, buildup, flakes, and other debris before shampoo is applied. This helps to prevent residual oils, debris, or flakes from remaining within your locs after shampooing.

If you have never used a pre-treatment on your scalp before, don't worry—you're not alone. In fact, I conducted a poll on my Instagram page, and over 70% of my IG family had never heard of or used a pre-treatment on their locs. And to be honest, I was shocked! But I understand that it's simply a matter of awareness.

One way to pre-cleanse your locs is with the shampoo you already have. As an example, when using a medicated shampoo as a pre-treatment, simply mix a quarter-sized amount of shampoo with half a cup of distilled water, then apply it to the scalp and root area of your locs. Let it sit for 5 to 10 minutes before proceeding with your regular cleansing regimen.

Not only does a pre-treatment help remove buildup that may be clogging the scalp, but it can also stimulate the hair follicles and encourage hair growth. So, pre-treatments are an optional yet beneficial step in your loc care routine.

Similarly, I believe conditioning is a key component to maintaining healthy locs. However, using conditioner on locs remains a widely debated topic. Let's explore whether conditioning locs is truly necessary—and, if so, how to do it correctly.

Using Conditioner on Locs

You'll hear recommendations to use conditioner on locs and you'll find just as many suggestions to avoid conditioner usage. My goal is to share the science behind conditioning and strengthening locs so that you can make the best decision for your journey.

Conditioning, at its core, involves applying an agent to the hair to restore strength and protect against damage. However, the type of conditioning agent suitable for locs may differ from what you might expect. While cream-based conditioners are commonly used for loose hair—especially in textured hair care—their application can negatively impact locs if not used properly.

Cream-based conditioners are designed to minimize tangles, reduce frizz, and smooth the hair, which aligns well with the needs of loose or relaxed hair. However, when it comes to locs, cream-based conditioners can slow down the locking process because they are formulated to detangle, and locs require tangling and matting in order to form.

After working with hundreds of locs throughout my career as a loctician, I've seen a clear difference between locs that are regularly conditioned and those that aren't.

- Locs that are never conditioned often experience **thinning along the shaft, frequent breakage, and chronic dryness**.

- Color-treated or bleached locs without proper conditioning tend to **shed excessively**—even when regularly moisturized.

- Many individuals mistakenly believe that daily moisturizing is enough, but without conditioning, their locs **remain dry, brittle, and prone to breakage**.

So, how can you condition your locs without the use of cream-based conditioners? *I'm glad you asked!* Let's explore a few alternatives to cream-based conditioners for locs.

Alternative Ways to Condition Locs

There are several ways to strengthen and condition your locs without using creamy conditioners. Here are three of my favorite methods: **herbal rinses, steam treatments, and hot oil treatments.**

Herbal Rinse: An herbal rinse is a specialized blend of herbs used to strengthen and nourish locs. It is prepared much like herbal tea and is poured throughout the hair and scalp after shampooing. Unlike cream-based conditioners, herbal rinses are <u>not</u> rinsed out. Instead, they allow the herbal nutrients to continue strengthening the hair. A well-formulated herbal rinse includes herbs that nourish the scalp, fortify the locs, and help prevent mold or mildew growth. A few common herbs that can be used individually or combined for a DIY herbal treatment include nettle, rosemary, chamomile, and burdock root.

Steam Treatment: A steam treatment is excellent for restoring softness and flexibility to your locs, especially if they've been feeling dehydrated. This method uses vaporized water (also known as steam) to penetrate the hair shaft and hydrate locs from the inside out. In fact, steam treatments are so beneficial to locs that you should aim to do one at least once every three months, regardless of whether you typically use it for conditioning after a cleansing session. You can invest in a hooded hair steamer for at home use or visit a professional for an in-salon steam treatment.

Hot Oil Treatment: A hot oil treatment can nourish a dry, dehydrated scalp and help seal moisture into locs. The key is using the right type of oil to avoid weighing down the hair or causing buildup. We will discuss oils for locs in the next chapter. But for now, keep in mind that hot oil treatments are for the scalp—so there's no need to drench your locs in oil!

Even with these alternatives for conditioning locs in mind, it's inevitable that some individuals, including locticians, will advocate for the use of cream-based conditioners on locs. While I don't oppose this practice, it's important to proceed with caution. When using a cream-based conditioner on locs, proper dilution is essential—mix 1 ounce of conditioner with 8 ounces of distilled water—and thoroughly rinse the cream-based conditioner out to avoid buildup. When done correctly, shampooing and conditioning can significantly improve the health and resilience of your locs.

"The highest version of you is the healthier version."
—Dr. Bobby Price

CHAPTER SEVEN

The Art of Moisturizing Locs

You're not alone if you've ever felt unsure about what "moisturize your hair" actually means. So, allow me to share my definition. **Moisturizing is the practice of replenishing moisture lost from your hair.** And to be very clear, moisture comes from one essential element: water. Also, your locs must be moisturized to remain healthy because dry locs cannot be healthy locs.

To better understand why proper moisturizing is important, imagine a box of uncooked spaghetti noodles. If you try to bend, or manipulate, dry noodles, what happens? *They break.* Now, think about those same noodles after they've been soaked in water. What happens when you try to bend them? *They remain intact and flexible.* This is a perfect example of **hair elasticity**—also known as your hair's flexibility. When hair is moisturized, it is stronger; when hair is dry, it is at its weakest.

Now, let's take it a step further. Imagine soaking those same uncooked spaghetti noodles in oil instead of water. Would they appear shiny and smooth? *Yes.* But would they still break as easily as the dry noodles? *Absolutely.*

This illustrates an often misunderstood fact: **oil is not a moisturizer.** Oil does not add moisture to the hair. However, it can support the moisturizing process by helping to seal in water (also known as moisture). This means moisturizing is a two-step process. First, the water, then the oil. But, before we get too caught up in the different types of oil, we first need to understand the foundation of what locs truly need—moisture.

Types of Moisturizers for Locs

Much of the confusion around moisturizing comes from the belief that all moisturizers are created equal. While the intention is always to add water to the hair, the type of moisturizer you use also impacts how it works and when it should be applied.

The moisturizers for locs generally fall into three main categories: **herbal, refreshing,** and **conditioning.**

- **Herbal Moisturizer.** An herbal moisturizer is formulated to hydrate and strengthen the hair and scalp. This type of moisturizer can be used on all types of locs at least 2 to 3 times per week. The power in an herbal moisturizer comes from the herbal extracts used in its formulation; such as dried roses, aloe vera, or rosemary. Rosewater is a common herbal moisturizer that many people use regularly. And one of my favorite herbal moisturizers is the *"Moisture Infusion"* by Crown Elements.

- **Refreshing Moisturizer.** A refreshing moisturizer is lightweight and primarily used to add fragrance to the hair. It's formulated with essential oils and can be used daily to "wake up" the hair. You can easily DIY a refreshing moisturizer by adding a few drops of your favorite essential oil to a spray bottle filled with distilled water.

- **Conditioning Moisturizer.** A conditioning moisturizer softens the hair and adds shine. These are typically water-based with the addition of carrier oils, proteins, and/or humectants. If you have color-treated or bleached locs, it's recommended to use a conditioning moisturizer at least 2 to 3 times per week.

Now, let's say you've found a good moisturizing routine, but a new moisturizer catches your eye. You might wonder if switching products will affect your hair's moisture balance. To help you make an informed choice, let's explore the best times to switch moisturizers.

When to Switch Moisturizers

I believe switching moisturizers should be intentional. Instead of jumping from product to product, consider why your hair needs a change. Here are a few common reasons to change your moisturizing routine:

- **Changes In Your Health.** Unfortunately, we live in a world where stress and illness can arise without warning. At the same time, our hair often tries to warn us of imbalances before we can fully recognize them. You may notice during a stressful life event or after an illness, that your usual moisturizer no longer works as effectively. In this case, performing a steam treatment and switching to an herbal moisturizer can help support your hair's health as your body recovers.

- **Changes In The Integrity Of Your Locs.** If you've recently colored your hair and noticed excessive dryness, it may be time to switch moisturizers and possibly your shampoo. Using a conditioning moisturizer and adding a moisturizing shampoo to your regimen would be recommended to help improve the strength of your hair.

- **Changes In The Weather.** If you live in a seasonal climate, your moisturizing needs will change throughout the year. For example, I live in Maryland, where winters are dry, and summers are humid. In this type of climate, you must be especially careful with moisturizers containing glycerin. Glycerin is a **humectant**, meaning it draws moisture from the environment into your hair. However, if there isn't an abundance of moisture in the air, it will pull moisture from your hair instead. So, in the summer, using an herbal moisturizer with glycerin would be beneficial, but in the winter, it could cause excessive dryness. To prevent this seasonal dryness, I often switch to an herbal moisturizer without glycerin in the winter. Given that, it's important to be mindful of your climate and adjust your moisturizer accordingly. This will help to ensure your locs are moisturized year round.

It is also important to note that when switching to a different moisturizer your hair needs time to adjust. Typically, three to four shampoo cycles is ideal. Notice I said shampoo cycles, not moisturizer usages.

Repeatedly giving the new moisturizer a clean slate to do its job will allow you to see its true potential. Whereas, applying a new moisturizer to dirty hair will give you mixed and unpredictable results. To be clear, by "dirty hair," I am referring to hair with residual product rather than implying that you or your locs are dirty. So, the next time you're considering switching moisturizers, do so with intention and start using it after you've recently cleansed your hair.

Now that we've covered the foundations of moisturizing and usage, let's explore the habits that will help maintain the hydration and moisture balance within your locs.

Hydration Habits for Moisture Balance

The difference between hydration and moisture in hair care comes down to internal state versus external application. Moisture, also known as water, is what you apply to your hair. Hydration, on the other hand, refers to your hair's ability to absorb and retain that moisture within its internal structure. Think of it this way: when your hair feels dry, you would say it is dehydrated, not unmoisturized. With that being said, the following practices will help you to keep your locs hydrated:

1. **Use Clarifying Shampoo.** The first step to moisturized locs always begins with your shampoo. But don't make the mistake of using only moisturizing shampoo when experiencing dryness. You need to clarify your hair first—removing all old product residue—to allow any future products (i.e. moisturizers) to work effectively.

2. **Don't Forget Your Steam Treatments.** Steam is one of the best treatments for moisturizing and conditioning your locs. You should visit a hair care professional at least once every three months for a steam treatment or you can invest in a hooded hair steamer for at-home use— *it really works wonders for locs, especially in colder months!*

3. **Hydrate From Within.** Staying hydrated is essential for overall health, and your hair is no exception. A general guideline is to consume at least half your body weight in ounces of water daily. Since your body is made up of more than 60% water, proper hydration helps lubricate your organs, muscles, and hair. You can also "eat" your water with foods like cucumbers, watermelon, celery, and oranges. **Always consult with your physician to ensure you're meeting your specific hydration needs based on your health and lifestyle.**

4. **Ditch The Shower Cap.** Unless you're trying to preserve a retwist or curly style, skip the shower cap! Instead, pin your hair up and allow some of the residual shower steam to penetrate your locs. However, this should only be done for morning showers—wetting or dampening your locs at night can lead to

mildew growth and unwanted odors.

5. **Stay Consistent.** Establish a weekly moisture routine for your locs. Begin with a water-based moisturizer, followed by an emollient oil to seal in moisture. It's recommended to moisturize at least 1 to 2 times per week to keep your locs properly moisturized.

Understanding the type(s) of moisturizer to use, when to switch to a new moisturizer, and how to keep your locs hydrated is important, but it's not the whole process.

Let's revisit the second step in the moisturizing process— applying oil.

The Truth About Oils and Your Scalp

Did you know that your body naturally produces oil for your hair? This natural oil, called sebum, is created by the sebaceous glands covering your scalp. Personally, I had no idea what sebum or sebaceous glands were until I had Sisterlocks™. For 21 years, I relied on oil and grease to make my hair and scalp *look* healthy. I lost count of how many times I heard the same solution shouted at me in my childhood home whenever my scalp looked dry: "Go put some oil on your scalp!"

So, when I was instructed by my loctician, after starting my Sisterlocks™, to avoid using oil, I was completely lost. Those first few months were rough—I had never experienced so much itching and flaking in my life. However, what my loctician called a *"scalp detoxification"* turned out to be one of the best things for my hair and scalp.

For over two decades, my scalp had never truly been allowed to produce its own natural oils. Without realizing it, I had been clogging my hair follicles, forcing my sebaceous glands to compete with the heavy oils and grease I constantly applied. But once I had no choice but to rely on my natural sebum, my scalp underwent a humbling yet necessary process of releasing years of oil buildup.

Unfortunately, many people don't recognize the damaging effects of clogged hair follicles until they start experiencing hair loss. So, to give your hair and scalp the best chance to thrive, it's important to understand why you're using oil and how to use it effectively.

The Difference Between Carrier Oil and Essential Oil

There are two primary types of oil used in hair care: carrier oils and essential oils.

Essential oils are highly concentrated extracts derived from various parts of plants, such as the leaves, seeds, roots, or bark. They offer therapeutic benefits, including antimicrobial and anti-inflammatory properties, as well as natural fragrance. Examples of essential oils include tea tree, peppermint, bergamot, and rosemary oil. However, due to their potency, essential oils should <u>never</u> be applied directly to the scalp. Instead, they must be properly diluted in a carrier oil or water to prevent irritation.

Carrier oils are extracted from the fatty parts of plants and vary in viscosity. Viscosity describes the thickness of the oil and ranges from light to heavy. Examples of carrier oils include olive, avocado, and apricot oil. When it comes to locs, choosing the right carrier oil is important for maintaining scalp health and preventing buildup. Lighter oils, such as grapeseed, closely mimic the scalp's natural sebum and are ideal for frequent usage without weighing down your locs. Heavier oils, like castor oil, can be beneficial for sealing in moisture but should be used sparingly to avoid buildup on the scalp and inside locs.

Choosing the Best Hair Oil

When selecting the right oil for your locs, I encourage you to remember that the primary role of oil is to support the moisturizing process. As an example, after applying a water-based moisturizer to your locs, the oil should act as a sealant, helping to slow moisture loss from the hair. With that being said, the thickness, or viscosity, of the oil is how you can determine which oil to use.

Lightweight Viscosity Oil:
Ideal for fine hair textures and microlocs. Can be blended in equal parts with a heavy oil to create a medium viscosity oil.
Examples include: *Argan Oil, Grapeseed Oil*

Medium Viscosity Oil:
Ideal type of oil to use. Suitable for all locs, hair types and textures.
Examples include: *Avocado Oil, Almond Oil*

Heavy Viscosity Oil:
Ideal for use on color-treated and/or bleached hair when combined with a lightweight or medium viscosity oil.
Examples include: *Castor Oil, Olive Oil*

For most loc'd hair, a medium-viscosity oil is the best choice. This viscosity allows moisture to dissipate naturally, making it easier to reapply a moisturizer and oil throughout the week without excessive buildup or greasiness.

Applying heavy oils too frequently can lead to both product and lint buildup. However, if your hair responds well to heavier oils, you can adjust the viscosity by blending them with lighter oils. For instance, if you prefer to use castor oil, mixing it with grapeseed oil creates a medium-viscosity oil blend that reduces the risk of attracting unwanted lint.

But if you're not interested in blending your own oils, pay close attention to ingredient labels. When reading product ingredient labels, the first three oils listed should not be heavy oils. This is advised because ingredients are often listed in order of concentration on the label.

Proper Hair Oil Application

It is possible to overuse or incorrectly apply oil to your locs and scalp. Instead of just saturating your scalp or hair with oil, ideally you want to first apply your water-based moisturizer evenly throughout your locs. Then, place a quarter-sized amount of oil in your hands, rub your hands together, and gently squeeze your oiled palms through the length of your locs. This will evenly distribute the oil through your locs.

Additionally, you can apply oil directly to your scalp after shampooing. Throughout the week it is best to allow your scalp to produce its own sebum rather than constantly compete with added oils.

By understanding the role of essential oils and carrier oils, knowing how to choose the right oil, and applying it correctly, you can nourish your scalp and support the overall health of your locs right at home.

"The truth is that only the most courageous are ever brought this far and deep into the unknown. The ones who are willing to face the darkness within themselves and the world to understand the level of light needed to move forward. You are here because you are one of the courageous ones."

Octavia F. Raheem, Pause,Rest, Be

CHAPTER EIGHT

Preventative Loc Care

Contrary to popular belief, locs are not cultivated from neglect. In fact, they require a level of care and protection best described as preventative.

Unfortunately, negative stereotypes about locs—combined with a lack of proper hair care education in our community and the influences of social media—have created a recipe for disaster. As a loctician, I have witnessed the devastating impact of inconsistent care countless times. But one story, in particular, stands out.

Imagine feeling hesitant to start locs because, for over 50 years, friends, family, and mainstream media have told you that locs were ugly, dirty, and unprofessional. Despite this negativity, in your late 50s, you decide to embrace your natural beauty and start locs on your salt-and-pepper hair. Because you want your locs to turn out right, you seek guidance from online resources. You stumble upon a channel that recommends a "hands-off" approach—no shampooing, no grooming, no styling. The recommended advice is to simply apply castor oil and leave your hair alone to grow into thick, strong locs. This method seems easy enough, and it aligns with what you've heard about locs your whole life. So you adopted this "hands-off" approach.

Now, fast forward one year.

I wish I could say this story had a happy ending. Unfortunately, the result was severe damage and neglect.

I met this woman after she came across my online blog and was shocked by how much care locs actually required. She immediately booked a consultation, confused about why her locs were thinning and her scalp felt irritated. What I found was heartbreaking—her locs were filled with buildup and her scalp was so inflamed that it had triggered hair loss. She had no idea what went wrong because she followed the advice she saw on a channel with thousands of views and subscribers.

It took several months of costly repairs to undo the damage and develop a proper loc care routine for her. She also had to unlearn years of poor hair habits. But once she understood the importance of proactive care versus reactive care, everything changed. She no longer felt insecure under the judgmental gaze of friends and family—she felt empowered—and her locs improved drastically!

With that in mind, I believe awareness is the first step towards proactive care. Being aware of common challenges and how to prevent them will give you the knowledge needed to make smarter choices for your hair's health.

In this chapter, we will explore how to avoid various types of buildup, common issues that affect locs, and the best accessories for protecting your hair.

Let's start with one of the biggest threats to healthy locs— *buildup.*

Understanding and Avoiding Buildup

There are five types of buildup that are most commonly found in locs: **product, lint, environmental, biological,** and **debris.** This is not to say that all locs will experience these types of buildup, but the effects of buildup can happen when you are not intentional and proactive in your at-home care practices.

Product Buildup

When hair products are not thoroughly rinsed out they can accumulate within the locs. This accumulation can lead to stiffness, heaviness, and even mold growth. Some of the most common products to cause buildup in locs include creams, butters, heavy oils, and waxes.

A common misconception is that by using products with natural ingredients you will avoid product buildup. However, even natural ingredients like shea butter can contribute to product buildup if not properly removed from the hair. While product selection is important, an effective cleansing routine is equally as important. If you do not thoroughly cleanse and rinse your locs, residual product will remain trapped, leading to buildup.

How to Avoid Product Buildup

You can avoid product buildup by using lightweight products specifically formulated for locs and always using clarifying shampoo when cleansing your hair. However, if buildup has already developed, a loc detox is necessary to remove the trapped residue within the locs.

After the detox, your locs should feel significantly lighter and refreshed. But don't overdo it— a loc detox is recommended no more than twice per year. It's also important to note that even if you don't see obvious signs of product buildup, an annual detox can help keep away excessive buildup and keep your locs feeling lightweight.

How to Perform a Loc Detox

This type of detoxification helps eliminate buildup caused by product, environmental matter, and other impurities. The process of detoxing your locs involves soaking your hair in a detoxifying solution that is intended to cleanse the hair, balance its natural pH, and break down mild to moderate buildup.

Recommended Ingredients:
- 2 gallons of alkaline water (as hot as you can comfortably withstand, near boiling is ideal)
- 3 tbsp lemon juice (filtered, pulp-free)
- ½ cup apple cider vinegar
- 2 tbsp alcohol-free witch hazel
- 1 tbsp sea salt

Instructions:
1. Prepare the detox bath by mixing all ingredients in a basin or sink.
2. Submerge your locs fully and soak for no more than 20 minutes.
3. Continuously squeeze the length of your locs during the soak to help release impurities.
4. Rinse thoroughly with warm water to remove any remaining residue. Proceed with your regular cleansing routine.

Lint Buildup

Lint is by far one of the most common types of buildup that affects locs. When oil is applied to the hair, locs can act like magnets for lint, dust, and small particles from the environment, leading to a grayish or dull appearance. Additionally, frequent contact with materials such as sweatshirts, scarves, cotton pillowcases, and towels increases the risk of lint buildup.

How to Avoid Lint Buildup:

Protecting your locs with a bonnet or scarf made of silk, satin, or a similar material is ideal. Wearing this type of head covering while sleeping and getting dressed minimizes contact with lint-prone fabrics. Also, after washing your hair, use a lint-free towel, such as a microfiber towel, rather than one made with cotton fibers.

Additionally, incorporating weekly loc brushing into your regimen can help minimize lint accumulation. Loc brushing involves using a soft-bristle brush on the length of your locs to dislodge trapped lint and fibers. However, you should be mindful of the type of bristles in the brush and avoid the root area to prevent damage. Hard-bristle brushes are not recommended, as they can disrupt the locking process or cause thinning.

How to Loc Brush: Use a soft-bristle loc brush and gently brush from root to tip, following the natural growth pattern of your locs.

Environmental Buildup

Environmental buildup comes from naturally-occuring materials in the air or directly present in the environments you frequent. The two most common culprits are dirt and soap scum. Dirt can be kicked up from the ground while you're outdoors, while soap scum often results from hard water. Unfortunately, many areas—especially in major U.S. cities—are plagued by hard water. Over time, an accumulation of environmental buildup in your locs can lead to brittle hair and dullness.

How to Avoid Environmental Buildup:

To prevent dirt from getting trapped in your locs, always wear a head covering when cleaning, dusting, or working outdoors.

To address soap scum, which forms due to excessive mineral deposits in the water, you have two options:

1. Use a chelating shampoo in your cleansing regimen to remove mineral deposits, and be sure to shampoo your locs at least twice per month.

2. Install a water filter on your showerhead or sink faucet to minimize hard water exposure. This is the most effective solution.

Biological Buildup

Biological buildup is a type of buildup that many people overlook, but most experience. This type of buildup occurs due to natural bodily secretions such as sweat, sebum, and shed skin cells accumulating in the locs. For example, when sweat combines with flakes and sebum, and they are not removed, it can lead to unpleasant odors and itching. In time, these biological matters become embedded within your locs, resulting in buildup.

How to Avoid Biological Buildup:

To avoid biological buildup in your locs, it's essential to understand your scalp and hair needs. Not everyone can go an entire three weeks without shampooing their locs—you may need to shampoo your hair weekly especially if you have a pre-existing scalp condition. Here are a few other suggestions to reduce biological buildup:

- Use a gentle, alcohol-free astringent spray on the scalp after sweating and especially after workouts to help reduce odor and itching. My favorite is the *"Pure Scalp"* by Crown Elements.

- Prevent mildew by drying your locs thoroughly whenever they are exposed to wetness—use a microfiber towel to absorb excess water.

- After shampooing your locs, strive to use a hooded dryer for at least 30 minutes and avoid prolonged air drying.

Debris Buildup

As your locs grow longer, buildup from debris such as makeup, food, and lotion becomes more common. It's often joked that once your locs extend past your shoulders, they get the first sip of any drink—because they're long enough to touch the cup before your lips!

So, here are a few preventative measures to minimize debris buildup:

How to Avoid Debris Buildup:

- Moisturize your hair before applying lotion to prevent unintentionally transferring lotion to your locs from your hands.

- Pull longer locs back while getting dressed to prevent lotion transfer.

- Secure locs out of the way while eating to avoid them dipping into food or beverages.

- Wear a scarf or headband when applying makeup to keep locs from coming in contact with it.

By being mindful and proactive in your loc care routine you can prevent buildup while keeping your locs looking and feeling their best.

Now, let's explore another common issue that can affect locs: **thinning**.

Identifying the Cause of Thinning and Hair Loss

Despite the "horror stories" you may hear on social media, locs do not cause your hair to thin. In fact, well maintained locs actually promote hair growth and length retention. However, thinning can happen during your loc journey, and understanding the common causes, recommended next steps, and when to seek professional help are important.

Thinning typically occurs along the hairline, the shaft of the locs, or at the roots. Common causes include, but are not limited to, medication, product buildup, hair color, tension, hormonal imbalances, dietary deficiencies, and stress.

Medication

It is not uncommon for certain prescription medications and medical treatments to cause hair thinning or hair loss as side effects. Unfortunately, when medication remains in your system, you have little to no control over the extent of hair loss you may experience. However, it is important to inform your hair care professional about any medications you're taking to prevent potential adverse reactions to hair products, as these reactions could further contribute to hair loss.

Product Buildup

Products that are not water-soluble do not work well with locs because they can accumulate and require harsh surfactants or shampoos to remove them. Specifically, products containing creams, butters, honey, or waxes tend to suffocate the locs from the inside out, leading to thinning and eventual breakage.

Hair Color

Any chemical process that alters the hair structure can cause weakness and thinning. Oftentimes, residual bleach or hair color gets left inside the locs. Especially when using an at home box color. When this hair color is not completely removed, the chemical can start to deteriorate the locs from the inside out, resulting in breakage.

Tension

Hair loss or thinning due to tension, commonly known as traction alopecia, can definitely happen with locs, even though it's most often associated with braids and weaves. Constantly pulling your locs into tight styles or using hair accessories that are too tight can damage your hair follicles, which in turn leads to thinning.

To protect your hairline from tension-related hair loss, keep these precautions in mind:

- Do not wear scarves or bonnets directly on your hairline; instead, position them on your forehead to reduce friction.

- Shampoo your hairline weekly if you use edge control on the front row of your locs.

- Do not retwist the hairline more than once per month.

- Avoid interlocking the edges when the hair is dry.

- Avoid styles that pull tightly or cause irritation.

Genetics & Hormonal Imbalances

The density of your hair is largely determined by your genetics. If hair loss or balding is common in your family, you may be predisposed to similar issues. While you cannot change your genes, you can minimize the early onset by maintaining a balanced diet and proactively monitoring your hormone and mineral levels with your physician.

Women with locs may also experience postpartum alopecia, a type of hair loss that occurs after pregnancy—typically between 4 to 7 months postpartum. According to the American Pregnancy Association, approximately 40% of women are affected by postpartum alopecia. With locs, this shedding can result in thinning at the roots, sometimes causing locs to fall out entirely or hang on by just a few strands. While there is little that can be done to stop this hormonally driven hair loss, it's important to continue prioritizing your overall wellness and trust that regrowth will come in time. If any locs do fall out, store them in a bag so they can be reattached once your new growth is healthy and strong enough to support them.

Dietary Deficiencies

Poor nutrition and lack of adequate water intake can largely contribute to thinning locs. A balanced diet rich in dark leafy greens, essential omega-3 and omega-6 fatty acids, and consuming at least half your body weight (in ounces) of water per day are essential for cultivating strong, healthy locs.

Stress

The effects of stress—whether physical or emotional—often manifest in our hair, typically in patches. If you're regularly impacted by moderate to severe stress, you may notice certain areas of your hair becoming fragile and weak. Reducing stress as much as possible is the best solution for thinning locs in these circumstances. Also, consider stress relieving activities like yoga, meditation, long walks, crocheting, reading, scalp massages, a technology detox, and drinking herbal tea.

Sadly, many people, particularly African-Americans, mistake stress for success. The cultural expectation to be twice as good and work twice as hard for equal or lesser recognition often takes a heavy toll.

The Price of Ignoring Self-Care

I recall starting microlocs on a teacher in her mid-20s. At the time, her hair was mostly coily with medium to high density, or in other words it was luxurious, strong and healthy. Which is why you wouldn't believe what her hair looked like just four years later. In that short time, she set her ambitions on becoming a principal. The demanding stress of her job, coupled with her lack of self-care, had a visible impact on her health and her hair.

During her salon appointments, I often addressed her stress before she did. I noticed bald spots in her crown and thinning locs throughout her hair—it was clear that stress was causing her hair loss. As much as I encouraged her to prioritize self-care through activities like walking, meditation, and moisturizing her locs; she always had an excuse. But the body has a way of forcing you to listen when you ignore its warning signs.

Eventually, she became so burdened by stress that she was forced to take a leave of absence from her school. With her health now her main priority, she started therapy, eliminated stress, and took her wellness seriously. Her hair thanked her. Her locs began to thicken and the thinning areas became less noticeable. Healthy hair became her norm rather than the exception. She later admitted that she never believed stress could affect her hair so much—until she saw it for herself. Fortunately, she now continues to use her hair as a measure of her well-being.

Personal Reflection:
Ask yourself— *What signs has my body been giving me?*

With all of the different ways thinning can show up in locs, plus the various factors that can cause it, identifying the root cause may not be something that you can assess on your own. You may need to seek the advice of a professional for a more accurate diagnosis.

Professional Guidance for Hair Loss

If you're experiencing thinning in your locs, it's important to visit a professional who can help you determine the cause(s) and recommend solutions. Some professionals you may want to consult include a dermatologist, trichologist, dietitian, or a certified holistic loctician.

- **Dermatologist** – A dermatologist is a doctor that specializes in skin, which includes the scalp. Dermatologists can offer treatments for hair loss, such as a microscopic scalp analysis, blood panels, and scalp biopsies. Additionally, they can provide the highest level of invasive care, including hair transplant surgery. However, the number of certified dermatologists who understand textured hair—especially locs—is very limited. A great resource to begin your search for a dermatologist is BlackDermDirectory.com.

- **Trichologist** – A trichologist specializes in scalp conditions and scalp disorders, including hair loss. Trichologists have more expertise and training in diagnosing and treating hair loss than salon professionals. However, it's imperative that you find a trichologist knowledgeable about textured hair and locs.

- **Dietitian** – A dietitian is trained to advise on food, nutrition, and overall health. Consulting a dietitian is especially helpful if you struggle with maintaining a balanced diet or have an underlying medical condition that may be contributing to hair loss. *You know what they say, "we are what we eat."*

- **Holistic Loctician** – A certified holistic loctician specializes in loc care and uses products that support scalp and hair health. In some cases, thinning can be managed with regular salon services and herbal remedies. However, it's important to note that **locticians, cosmetologists, and other salon professionals are not licensed to diagnose scalp conditions or scalp disorders**—only dermatologists and trichologists have the medical training to do so. To find a certified holistic loctician, visit certifiedlocticians.com

Taking Action to Repair Thinning Locs

One of the biggest mistakes people make when their locs start thinning is assuming that a single product—whether a vitamin, oil, or shampoo—will solve all their issues. However, addressing thinning locs is most effective when approached holistically, helping to prevent further hair loss and minimize the risk of future thinning.

Once the cause is identified and a plan is in place, consistency becomes key. While it sounds simple, staying consistent is often the hardest part for most people. But sticking to your treatment plan will offer the best results. You may also need to repair or reinforce locs that have already thinned.

- **Thinning along the shaft** can generally be repaired using human afro kinky hair and a micro crochet needle.

- **Thinning at the roots** may require releasing (cutting) the affected loc(s). Although some may suggest combining locs at the roots, instead of cutting them, this is best determined by the part-to-loc ratio discussed in chapter 3. If the base cannot support the weight of two locs combined, this will only lead to further thinning.

Ultimately, I strongly encourage you to seek professional help as soon as possible. Avoid the temptation to rely on social media for advice—you'll often find countless quick fixes that lead to an endless cycle of trial and error. As Dr. Yolanda Lenzy, a renowned dermatologist and hair loss expert, says: **"Time is follicles."** So, the sooner you take action, the greater your chances of saving your locs.

Now that we've covered thinning and the types of buildup let's shift to understanding how accessories can impact your locs.

Choosing Accessories That Protect Locs

Locs are low-maintenance in the sense that they don't require many tools or accessories for upkeep. Three of the most common accessories for locs include **loc jewelry, hair bonnets, and hair ties.** In this section, we'll explore how each one impacts loc'd hair and how to wear them without causing damage.

Loc Jewelry

Loc jewelry can be worn with all types of locs, from Sisterlocks™ to freeform locs. However, the term "loc jewelry" covers a broad range of adornments. I prefer to categorize loc jewelry as **permanent** and **temporary**, so that you can understand how the type you choose impacts your locs.

- **Permanent loc jewelry** is typically attached by threading, meaning it is woven into the locs. You can wear it while showering or grooming your locs. However, if you maintain your locs with interlocking, your options for permanent jewelry are more limited. This is because the permanent jewelry would need to pass through the roots during grooming, which can be difficult—especially if, for example, you have a cowrie shell sewn at the end of your loc. And due to the permanence of this adornment, careful precautions must be taken if you decide to attempt removal.

- **Temporary loc jewelry** is the more common option, as it can be easily removed and reattached. This flexibility is beneficial if you shampoo frequently and want to prevent tarnishing or if you enjoy switching which of your locs are adorned. However, be mindful of the materials used. Just like rings for your fingers—copper, silver, and brass jewelry—can cause discoloration. Meaning a green band can form on your locs as a result of the chemical reaction between the pH of your hair, hair products, and the metal oxidizing. To avoid this, it is best to remove loc jewelry before shampooing or applying products. Alternatively, you could opt for stainless steel or gold loc jewelry, which is resistant to tarnishing.

Regardless of the type of loc jewelry you choose, **the maturity of your locs matters most**. It is strongly recommended **NOT** to wear loc jewelry during the first six months of your loc journey. Wearing jewelry too early can create chokeholds in your locs or lead to thin spots along the shaft.

So, before you invest in loc jewelry, make sure you consider how mature your locs are, how you plan to groom your locs, and any potential skin and hair reactions to different metals.

Bonnet

A bonnet made of satin, silk, or a similar material is excellent for protecting locs at night and maintaining hairstyles. Covering your locs at night while you sleep helps retain moisture in your hair, preventing dryness often caused by cotton sheets and pillowcases.

The size of a bonnet is typically spacious enough to accommodate voluminous hairstyles such as curls and updos. However, if you've recently started your loc journey, keep in mind that the extra space in a bonnet allows your locs to move freely at night, which can lead to increased frizz—especially for fine textures, and curly or wavy hair types. An alternative to wearing a bonnet is to wear a scarf that ties securely and fits snugly around your head. This will minimize hair movement, which in turn will help to reduce frizz.

I also highly recommend that you avoid wearing scarves or bonnets directly on your hairline. Instead, position them on your forehead to prevent excessive friction that could lead to thinning edges.

Hair Ties

There have been several improvements to this category in recent years. However, if you asked me a few years ago about the different types of hair ties for locs, I probably would have mentioned two—a scrunchie and a headband—the classics. They are affordable and, dare I say, dispensable. However, I've since discovered several hair ties that are better suited for specific lengths of locs, making casual wear and everyday styling tension-free. Here are my top three hair ties for locs:

1. **Scrunchie.** These are a dime a dozen— *well, not literally, but close!* They're simple, easy to use, and available in a range of colors. However, one major downside is their limited stretch. As

your locs increase in size and grow longer, scrunchies are more likely to snap, and/or not provide enough hold for styling. For that reason, I don't recommend using scrunchies beyond the time when your locs reach shoulder-length.

2. **Spiral Cord Elastic.** These hair ties are especially useful once your locs reach shoulder length. They're comfortable, stretchy, and affordable, with a no-tension hold. Personally, I also really liked that the size of my locs fit into the "grooves" of the cords. For that reason, spiral cord elastics work well for both low and high ponytails. But as your locs continue to grow longer and heavier, spiral cord elastics may not provide enough support. For instance, using a spiral cord elastic for a high ponytail on locs that are mid-back length will cause the ponytail to fall within minutes.

3. **Snappee™.** This hair tie is an incredible creation for locs of all sizes! The comfort is unmatched, and I love that I could easily create a high ponytail even when my locs nearly reached my lower back. And on top of that, you can daisy-chain multiple Snappee™ hair ties together to expand their width. So it goes without saying— *I highly recommend these for locs of all lengths.*

When it comes down to it, maintaining healthy locs involves taking a proactive approach to common issues like buildup and less common occurrences like thinning. By understanding the types of buildup that can affect your locs and addressing them promptly, you can cultivate strong, healthy locs throughout your journey. Also, incorporating proactive techniques like loc brushing and detox treatments will help keep your locs looking and feeling their best. With preventative care, your locs will grow and thrive, representing an outer reflection of your dedication to self-care and total body wellness.

"Drink Your Water. Protect Your Energy.
Moisturize Your Hair. Mind Your Business."
—The Digital Loctician

CHAPTER NINE

Setting Intentions For Your Loc Journey

At some point in your loc journey, I can almost guarantee that you'll hear locs described as a plant—and I believe that analogy to be true. Just like a plant, locs require patience, care, and light to thrive. And just as you wouldn't sow a seed and expect it to sprout overnight, you shouldn't begin your loc journey expecting perfection. But in today's society, where social media keeps us constantly "connected," *loc envy* can easily show up to steal your light. But it's important to remember that just as no two plants grow identically, no two sets of locs will ever be the same. Every journey is different. And loc envy distracts you from appreciating your own unique journey. This is why I strongly encourage you to set the following three intentions for your loc journey: to protect your peace, to celebrate your growth, and to always remember your "why." Just like roots nourish a plant, these intentions will help keep you grounded through moments of comparison, self-doubt, and on those days when you question your own growth.

Protect Your Peace

Nowadays, with so much of our daily lives broadcasted online, it's easy to admire someone else's locs on your feed and wish yours looked the same—even without knowing how their journey began or what they've faced along the way. But when we idolize someone else's journey, we unintentionally diminish our own progress and growth. Because truthfully, we don't see the reality behind the highlight reel that is projected online; we take what we see online at face value and overlook the challenges behind them. This kind of comparison—or loc envy—is a slippery slope. The moment you start measuring your locs against someone else's, you rob yourself of the beauty in your own transformation. As I've shared before, comparison is the thief of joy. And while letting go of comparison is easier said than done, it is possible. That's why setting an intention to protect your peace should be one of the first steps in your loc journey—or something you begin practicing right away if you've already started your locs.

Protecting your peace begins with limiting your exposure to content that makes you question your progress. You may not even realize how much these social media pages are affecting you, but constantly scrolling through imagery of other people's hair can unconsciously convince you that yours isn't enough. So when you notice yourself comparing, take a break. Unfollow, mute, or scroll past those posts to maintain your self-confidence, and peace of mind.

This also applies to real-life interactions with family, friends, co-workers, or even strangers. Gentle reminder: you do not have to accept anyone's judgments or unsolicited opinions about your journey. If someone's comments make you feel small, I encourage you to speak up for yourself. That doesn't mean trying to change their views or engaging in a conflict. Instead, shift the narrative their words create in your mind. One powerful way to do this is through affirmations. Speak them daily—and especially on days when someone tries to speak anything other than love into your spirit. Stand in front of a mirror and say these words aloud:

I define my beauty and nobody else.

I am gifted with naturally beautiful hair.

I radiate confidence and courage.

I am committed to learning more about myself through my journey.

As you continue to affirm yourself and grow in confidence, you'll become more skilled at letting go of judgment. Essentially, holding the intention to protect your peace keeps you from internalizing criticism and reminds you that your journey is enough—just as it is.

Celebrate Your Growth

The second intention to set on your loc journey is to celebrate your growth. One of the best ways to do this is by documenting your progress. I strongly encourage you to take pictures of your locs at different stages. There will be times when you feel like your hair isn't growing or locking fast enough, but looking back at old photos will show you just how much transformation has taken place. The changes may be gradual or subtle, but they are real. Your hair is evolving. Your locs are forming. Your journey is unfolding exactly as it should—in the timing and ways that are uniquely meant for you.

You can also create a ritual around the day you began your loc journey. Your *locversary*—as it is affectionately called—is the perfect opportunity to reflect on the past year; including how much you've grown and how far you've come. On your locversary, you might celebrate by writing a letter to yourself, creating a reflective video or social media post about your past year, or treating yourself to professional services—especially if you usually maintain your own locs. In this way, it becomes a personal milestone, one that honors both your outer and inner growth. When you hold the intention to celebrate your growth, you shift your perspective.

Instead of waiting for your locs to reach a certain length or look a specific way, you begin appreciating the transformation itself. And when you do that, you come face-to-face with the beauty that was always there just waiting for you to see it.

Remember Your Why

Finally, set an intention to always remind yourself why you started. *Was it for convenience? Were you ready to let go of wigs, weaves, flat irons, or relaxers? Maybe it was due to a health concern or was an effort to protect the health of your hair. Or perhaps you simply felt called to embrace a new and different look.* Whatever your reason, remember that this journey is yours alone. And you deserve this journey—this collection of experiences that shift your perspective, challenge your self-image, and lead you toward self-discovery.

As setbacks or challenges arise or mainstream trends shift, it becomes even more important to honor your "why." This is how you stay grounded—by following your heart rather than someone else's definition of beauty, success, or worth. Your why is the guiding light along your journey because it's inevitable that *how* you show up in this world will evolve over time. Staying connected to your why creates space for curiosity. And it's through curiosity that you find the permission and courage to show up as your most authentic self. In allowing yourself to trust this process of unlearning and redefining, free from judgement or expectations, you'll uncover a reflection that is uniquely, unapologetically yours.

And that is more than enough.

Index

Acknowledgements

Writing this book has been a practice in patience, determination, love, connection, and commitment—all qualities I thank God for the opportunity to embody. At the same time, I am eternally grateful for Torey, my husband. He saw the vision before I did. He saw my passion for empowering others and made the time to transcribe the knowledge I shared with my clients and in my videos—the backbone of this book. Fast forward nearly a decade later, and I was able to wrap my expertise with experience. You're holding the manifestation of that vision.

I am also so, so, so grateful for my digital community. It was there that I found solace when embracing my natural hair (and beauty) was met with resistance in my physical space. Online, I felt supported. To everyone who has followed my journey through the years—from CurlyNuGrowth to the Digital Loctician®—and every stage and evolution in between: I truly appreciate you for supporting, challenging, and encouraging me!

A special thank you to my Nana—for all the months you spent reading and learning about locs to help me edit my manuscript. Your presence and words of encouragement meant the world to me throughout the process!

To Mango & Papaya—thank you for believing in me and always being down to listen as I read chapters or sent requests for feedback—especially in the middle of the night and first thing in the morning (because parenting!).

To my children—thank you for your grace in all the moments I declined the opportunity to play because "Mommy has to finish her book." Your understanding allowed this—*my first published book*—to exist in the world.

To my mother—*"Look what I did, Mom!"* Thank you for believing in me and trusting my ability to fulfill my purpose in the world. And shoutout to my (step)dad for telling any and every person you saw with natural hair or locs to "check out my daughter's website!"—your support has always been felt.

Thank you, Auntie, for inviting me into your salon space and having the patience to teach me. *You changed my life!*

To all the salon guests who invited me along their journey and shared space with me in ways that allowed my salon to be a fertile ground for healing and growth—thank you. I am truly honored to have served you.

And last, but certainly not least, thank YOU for reading this guide and trusting me to share my wisdom with you. Because of you, I am.

About the Author

Jocelyn Reneé is a licensed cosmetologist, certified loctician, registered yoga teacher, and the founder of Crown Elements®, a holistic hair care company established in 2017. With roots in the beauty industry dating back to childhood—braiding hair at age 9 and working as a salon assistant by 12—she has cultivated over two decades of hands-on experience in natural hair care, wellness, and entrepreneurship.

A graduate of the Aveda Institute with training in both cosmetology science and ayurvedic wellness, Jocelyn has operated her own salon suite, mentored aspiring locticians, and provided expert care to hundreds of clients on their loc journeys. Known online as the *Digital Loctician®*, she has built a thriving platform that reaches more than 100,000 people through social media and her long-standing blog. What began as a space to celebrate the beauty of natural hair has grown into a trusted educational resource for loc care, product guidance, and holistic living.

At the heart of her work is a simple but powerful belief: *love exists in her hands*. Through writing, teaching, and intentional living, Jocelyn empowers others to redefine beauty on their own terms and courageously choose daily acts of self-care as a path to wellbeing.

She currently resides in Maryland, with her husband and three children, where she continues to educate, inspire, and create with intention.

www.ingramcontent.com/pod-product-compliance
Lightning Source LLC
Chambersburg PA
CBHW040854120626

46551CB00001B/17